I0408125

S. Hrg. 114–582

ASSESSING THE SECURITY OF OUR CRITICAL TRANSPORTATION INFRASTRUCTURE

HEARING

BEFORE THE

SUBCOMMITTEE ON SURFACE TRANSPORTATION AND MERCHANT MARINE INFRASTRUCTURE, SAFETY AND SECURITY

OF THE

COMMITTEE ON COMMERCE, SCIENCE, AND TRANSPORTATION UNITED STATES SENATE

ONE HUNDRED FOURTEENTH CONGRESS

SECOND SESSION

DECEMBER 7, 2016

Printed for the use of the Committee on Commerce, Science, and Transportation

U.S. GOVERNMENT PUBLISHING OFFICE

24–732 PDF   WASHINGTON : 2017

For sale by the Superintendent of Documents, U.S. Government Publishing Office
Internet: bookstore.gpo.gov   Phone: toll free (866) 512–1800; DC area (202) 512–1800
Fax: (202) 512–2104   Mail: Stop IDCC, Washington, DC 20402–0001

CONTENTS

ASSESSING THE SECURITY OF OUR CRITICAL TRANSPORTATION INFRASTRUCTURE

WEDNESDAY, DECEMBER 7, 2016

U.S. SENATE,
SUBCOMMITTEE ON SURFACE TRANSPORTATION AND
MERCHANT MARINE INFRASTRUCTURE, SAFETY, AND SECURITY,
COMMITTEE ON COMMERCE, SCIENCE, AND TRANSPORTATION,
Washington, DC.

The Subcommittee met, pursuant to notice, at 2:40 p.m. in room SR–253, Senate Russell Office Building, Hon. Deb Fischer, Chairman of the Subcommittee, presiding.

Present: Senators Fischer [presiding], Booker, Nelson, McCaskill, Klobuchar, and Blumenthal.

OPENING STATEMENT OF HON. DEB FISCHER, U.S. SENATOR FROM NEBRASKA

Senator FISCHER. Good afternoon. I am pleased to convene the Senate Subcommittee on Surface Transportation and Merchant Marine Infrastructure, Safety, and Security, for our last subcommittee hearing of 2016 titled "Assessing the Security of Our Critical Transportation Infrastructure."

Securing our Nation's transportation system is critical to keeping Americans safe. Over the past year, we've seen an increasing threat of terrorism to vital surface transportation networks. On September 17, a bomb exploded in New York City's Chelsea neighborhood injuring 31 people. Two days later, police in Elizabeth, New Jersey, removed from a public trash can a backpack filled with pipe bombs. The devices were discovered near the town's train station. Fortunately, no one was killed in either bombing.

But earlier this year, in Nice, France, a member of ISIL drove a commercial truck into a crowded promenade, killing 84 people. And in March, 16 individuals were killed in a bomb blast at a metro station in Brussels. These tragic events underscore a dangerous reality. Our surface transportation, rail, ports, pipelines, and mass transit systems are at serious risk of attack.

Unlike TSA aviation security checkpoints at our airports, TSA does not directly manage surface transportation security. Instead, TSA is responsible for providing guidance, oversight, intelligence, and assistance to system operators and law enforcement so that they can ensure security across our Nation's surface transportation network.

However, recent reports by the Office of the Inspector General of the Department of Homeland Security have questioned the TSA's management of our Nation's surface transportation security programs and resources. A September 2016 IG report found that over-sight of a critical TSA port access program, otherwise known as TWIC, had inadequate oversight. TWIC impacts nearly 3.5 million port and freight workers. The IG's office found that the program's fraud detection techniques were not monitored, and key internal controls were missing from the terrorism vetting process.

A second, even more alarming IG report from September found that TSA lacks an intelligence-driven, risk-based security strategy that informs security and resource decisions across all transportation modes, beyond aviation. The report further noted that TSA lacks a formal process to incorporate risk in budget formulation decisions. The TSA's annual budget is approximately $7.3 billion.

When TSA Administrator Peter Neffenger testified earlier this year before this committee, he pointed out that TSA spends just 3 percent of its budget on surface transportation security initiatives. This fact may come as a surprise to most Americans. Congress must evaluate the adequacy of these resources and demand that they be spent based on the threat risk to our transportation network. It's clear that our ports, highways, pipelines, and railways are at risk. Today's hearing convenes a panel of multimodal stakeholders and experts to discuss how we can enhance the security of our transportation system and ensure that the TSA is effective.

This fall, Chairman Thune, Ranking Member Nelson, Senator Booker, and I introduced the bipartisan Surface Transportation and Maritime Security Act to address these concerns. This comprehensive bill would instruct the TSA to establish risk-based budgeting, expand the highly effective K–9 explosive detection teams for surface transportation, and authorize computer vetting systems for passenger networks. Among other provisions, this important legislation would address management inefficiencies raised by the Inspector General as it relates to the TWIC program.

In May 2015, the Senate Commerce Committee passed the Essential Worker Identification Credential Assessment Act, which compels the TSA to fully assess the TWIC program and work with the Inspector General to resolve vetting, oversight, and other major security loopholes.

I am pleased to convene this hearing with the Inspector General of the Department of Homeland Security and leading experts from the pipeline, trucking, and passenger rail sectors. I look forward to learning more about how you advance all aspects of security in your daily operations and how we can work together to strengthen our transportation security.

I would now like to invite my colleague and this subcommittee's Ranking Member, Senator Cory Booker, to offer any opening remarks.

Senator Booker?

STATEMENT OF HON. CORY BOOKER,
U.S. SENATOR FROM NEW JERSEY

Senator BOOKER. Thank you so much, Chairwoman Fischer, for holding yet another very important hearing on surface transportation, in general, surface transportation security, in particular. I really look forward to hearing from all the witnesses.

The focus of this hearing is clearly on transportation security. But I just want to take a moment to speak about transportation safety. The Senate is now considering a CR, which, among other provisions, includes a dangerous rollback in truck safety that will have the effect of allowing truck drivers to work more hours and get less rest. Some colleagues and I have fought this battle time and time again, but it continues to remain an uphill battle.

The data is chilling. Now, there are 4,000 people who lose their lives to large truck accidents each year, and over 100,000 people are injured. It is paramount that Congress works together in a deliberative way, having a discussion on what is one of the monumental areas in which people are dying in America. The numbers we're talking about represent a plane crash each week in America. That's how many people are dying, and the situation is not getting better. It's actually getting worse. There's a 4.4 percent increase in accidents from 2014 to 2015.

We have a lot of good minds on this, from industry to activists to Senators on both sides of the aisle. We should be discussing this issue in the regular course of business, not flipping into a CR a rollback of these restrictions. It may be business as usual in the U.S. Senate, but it's something I just cannot accept or at least let go by quietly.

I spent time with the victims of these accidents, the tragedy that is being visited upon family after family, day after day, and it irks me that this is something that we can prevent, working together. I'm shocked and saddened that the data has not compelled more action on this issue.

The threat of a security challenge or a terrorist attack is real, and while I'm pleased that we're discussing those issues today, I hope we will double down on our commitment to explore basic road safety issues in the upcoming year and find ways to make our highways safer for all Americans. We can coexist. We can make sure business is done and families are safe.

Now, when it comes to security threats as a whole, New Jersey is often a prime target, given the density of our location. Over the course of a weekend this past September, as the Chairwoman noted, a series of attacks occurred in my home state and the surrounding region. In Seaside Park, New Jersey, an improvised device exploded in a garbage can near the course of a charity race. It could have been devastating and, fortunately, was not.

In Manhattan, just 12 miles from where I live, an explosion injured 30 people on a crowded sidewalk in Chelsea. Finally, a bag of explosives were found near a train station in Elizabeth, New Jersey, just about a mile from where I live.

These planned attacks are a stark reminder of how quickly our relative peace can be shattered and how we must ensure that we are adapting to new threats. This is particularly true for our surface transportation systems, where transit and passenger rail move millions of people every single day.

The 9/11 Commission, chaired by former New Jersey Governor Tom Kean, recognized this challenge and identified that terrorists may turn their attention from air to rail and transit stations as targets. Unfortunately, nearly a decade after we passed the implementation of recommendations of the 9/11 Commission Act, we are still, still waiting on TSA to complete many of the recommendations. That is unacceptable.

And it's not just rail and transit. The Commission also highlighted the need to secure the major ports, pipelines, bridges, and tunnels. With thousands of containers moving in and out of the port area in which I live and many millions of Americans do, hazardous materials moving through our pipelines, and cargo moving on trucks and rails across the country, the transportation network is vast and open. There is a serious security challenge.

The transportation industry is a backbone of our economy. A catastrophic failure of our transportation system could have serious economic consequences, not to mention the tragic loss of life, with terrorists focused on these soft targets.

For example, the Hudson River Tunnel, which connects northern New Jersey to midtown Manhattan, carries approximately 200,000 passengers every day. It is a vital economic artery for the region and a critical evacuation route for Manhattan in the event of a terrorist attack. I remember what happened after 9/11 just trying to get people out of Manhattan and first responders in.

Because the tunnel lacks redundancy, a terrorist attack in the tunnel would be catastrophic and would have long-term economic consequences for the Nation. We know the billions of dollars of economic loss just when New Jersey transit or Northeast Corridor rail systems are shut down. Bi-state efforts are currently underway to advance the Gateway Program, which would add a critical layer of redundancy across the busiest river crossing in the United States of America. I'm hopeful that we will take the necessary action to realize the security and mobility benefits that a new tunnel would offer.

In addition, we must continue to find new ways to adapt and meet the ever-challenging threats to our transportation system. That's why I've joined with Chairman Thune, Ranking Member Nelson, and Senator Fischer to introduce the Surface Transportation and Maritime Security Act, another example of our bipartisan efforts to make America safer. This bill will take steps to close the gap in our security and provide additional resources to enhance security across our transportation system.

Again, I look forward to hearing from the witnesses today. I'm grateful that Chief Belfiore is here as well, in particular. We have a lot of work to do. We can do more, and we must do more to meet the threats that are facing our nation's surface transportation.

Thank you very much.

Senator FISCHER. Thank you, Senator Booker.

I would just like to say it has been a pleasure to serve on this committee with Senator Booker. In the last two years, we have accomplished quite a bit. We've worked together in that bipartisan manner, looking for issues that we can agree upon that are really going to help the people of this country.

And it has been a pleasure, sir, to work with you.

I think we've had about 16 hearings over 2 years, either here in Washington or outside of Washington around this country, and Senator Booker has been a wonderful partner on every single issue that we've worked on.

At this time, I would like to introduce the panel one by one and have you give your statements before the Committee. We'll begin with the Honorable John Roth, who is the Inspector General of the United States Department of Homeland Security.

Welcome, sir.

STATEMENT OF HON. BILL NELSON, U.S. SENATOR FROM FLORIDA

Senator NELSON. Madam Chairman, may I enter an opening statement?

Senator FISCHER. Oh, I apologize, Ranking Member Nelson. I did not see you come in. Please give us your opening statement.

Senator NELSON. I'll just enter the opening statement in the record.

[The prepared statement of Senator Nelson follows:]

PREPARED STATEMENT OF HON. BILL NELSON, U.S. SENATOR FROM FLORIDA

I want to thank Chairman Fischer and Ranking Member Booker for calling this hearing about protecting our Nation's surface transportation networks from terrorist attacks.

A series of attacks over the last year or so—from attacks in France and Belgium to those right here in the U.S.—have rung the alarm bell that we cannot be complacent.

Transportation remains an attractive target for terrorists.

This Committee has heard that call. Last year, the Committee took an important step to improve aviation security by moving the Airport Security Enhancement and Oversight Act of 2015.

This bill took common sense steps to prevent an insider threat to our aviation system by improving the background checks for aviation workers. It also increased random physical screenings and covert, red-team testing.

And while these steps were essential, the threat is ever changing.

I am concerned that our current strategy does not sufficiently address the vulnerabilities exposed in Brussels and in the pipe bomb attacks in New York and New Jersey.

Those incidents highlighted the vulnerability of our surface transportation networks.

That is why I worked with Chairman Thune and Senators Fischer and Booker to introduce the Surface Transportation and Maritime Security Act.

The legislation addresses deficiencies in TSA's efforts to secure our rail, transit, highway, port and freight transportation systems.

It also responds to recent concerns raised by the Department of Homeland Security Inspector General.

The Inspector General found that TSA has yet to complete several important and overdue requirement from the recommendations of the 9/11 Commission which were enacted into law in 2007.

For example, it's been 8 years, and TSA has yet to develop rules to ensure that surface transportation workers have sufficient security training, or that railroads have clear standards for their security plans.

In addition, the Inspector General identified serious gaps in TSA's program to provide credentials for workers accessing secure areas of ports.

Fifteen years after TSA first established its Transportation Worker Identification Credential program, the agency still struggles to prevent fraud in the vetting of workers.

This legislation addresses deficiencies identified by the Inspector General and requires TSA to make changes.

Importantly, the legislation also takes steps to respond to the recent pipe bomb attacks by immediately adding 70 additional canine teams.

It also gives TSA the ability to add up to 200 teams over time.

Canine teams provide a power psychological and physical deterrent to potential threats.

They also have an unparalleled ability to identify detect explosives.

I believe it's time to reexamine our transportation security strategy and refocus our efforts, and this legislation helps us get there.

I want to thank the witnesses for coming today and I look forward to hearing from you on these issues.

Senator FISCHER. And we are pleased to welcome you to the Committee hearing today.

Senator NELSON. Yes, ma'am.

Mr. Roth?

STATEMENT OF HON. JOHN ROTH, INSPECTOR GENERAL, U.S. DEPARTMENT OF HOMELAND SECURITY

Mr. ROTH. Chairwoman Fischer, Ranking Member Booker, and members of the Subcommittee, thank you for inviting me here to testify today.

TSA has a broad responsibility to oversee and regulate surface transportation: highway, freight and passenger rail, mass transit, and pipelines, as well as port security. However, TSA's budget allocates most of its resources to air passenger screening and dedicates only a small portion, roughly about 2 percent, to vulnerable areas of surface transportation.

Recently, our office has published three reports that identify significant weaknesses in TSA's ability to secure surface transportation in the Nation's maritime facilities and vessels. First, we issued a report that found that TSA does not have an intelligence-driven, risk-based security strategy to inform security and budget needs across all types of transportation.

In 2011, TSA began publicizing that it uses an intelligence-driven, risk-based approach across all transportation modes. However, in fact, TSA incorporates a risk-based approach only in aviation and really only at the checkpoint. Additionally, they do not have a budget process that would incorporate risk into its budget decisions or resource allocations.

TSA is working to create a consolidated risk-based security strategy across all transportation modes. However, notwithstanding the fact that they've been working on this for a considerable amount of time, they do not intend to provide us with a risk-based security strategy until the last quarter of 2017.

The second report that we issued found that TSA has failed to develop and implement regulations governing passenger rail security required more than 9 years ago. Specifically, although required to by the implementing recommendations of the 9/11 Commission Act of 2007, TSA neither identified high-risk carriers nor issued regulations requiring those carriers to conduct vulnerability assessment and implement DHS-approved security plans.

TSA also did not issue regulations that would require a railroad security training program. Further, unlike aviation and maritime port workers, TSA has not developed regulations requiring security background checks for rail workers. TSA has just submitted a Notice of Proposed Rulemaking on one rule to the *Federal Register*. However, they won't even commit to a timeline as to when they will move the other two regulations forward.

The third report we issued found that TSA is missing key internal controls in the Transportation Worker Identification Credential Program, known by its acronym, TWIC. The background check for TWIC includes a check for immigration, criminal, and terrorist-related offenses that would preclude someone from being granted unescorted access to secure facilities at seaports. Our review found that TSA did not adequately integrate the security measures intended to identify fraudulent applications into the background check process. This was the case, notwithstanding the fact, that a Government Accountability report found the same problems 5 years ago.

We determined that TSA's lack of oversight was the primary reason that the TWIC background check process had so many control weaknesses. At the time of our review, the TWIC background check process was divided among multiple program offices, so no single entity had complete oversight and authority over the program. Furthermore, the lead program office for the program lacked key metrics to measure TSA's success in achieving TWIC program core objectives.

Many of the issues I've discussed today are addressed in S. 3379, the Surface Transportation and Maritime Security Act. We believe that, if enacted, this legislation will direct numerous improvements to our Nation's security. However, I must emphasize that the Department and TSA have demonstrated over time, a pattern of being dismissive and lax on implementing requirements related to non-aviation security. Under these circumstances, change will require significant oversight by Congress, by my office, and the Controller General to ensure that TSA and the Department take timely actions to implement these improvements.

Madam Chairman, this concludes my testimony. I would welcome any questions you or other members of the Committee may have.

[The prepared statement of Mr. Roth follows:]

DHS OIG HIGHLIGHTS

ASSESSING THE SECURITY OF OUR CRITICAL SURFACE TRANSPORTATION INFRASTRUCTURE

Why We Did This

The audits discussed in this testimony are part of our ongoing oversight of the Transportation Security Administration (TSA). Our reviews are designed to ensure efficiency and effectiveness of TSA operations in order to fulfill both aviation and non-aviation-related missions.

What We Recommend

We made numerous recommendations to TSA in our audit reports discussed in this testimony.

What We Found

TSA has many responsibilities in addition to providing security for our Nation's aviation passengers—including highway, freight and passenger rail, mass transit, port security, and pipelines. However, TSA has not considered these areas a priority, thus exposing the traveling public and sensitive infrastructure to additional risk. This testimony highlights several recent audits of TSA's non-aviation security-related missions. Our findings include:

- TSA lacks an intelligence-driven, risk-based security strategy that informs security and resource decisions across all modes of transportation.
- TSA has not fully implemented internal controls that strengthen the reliability of port worker background checks.
- TSA has not implemented regulations governing passenger rail security, established a rail training program, nor conducted security background checks of frontline rail employees.
- We believe that the *Surface Transportation and Maritime Security Act*, if enacted, will assist in addressing a number of the challenges facing the Depart-

ment and direct TSA to correct significant deficiencies in its programs and operations.

Agency Comments

We issued 10 recommendations that TSA concurred with and, in most cases, has begun implementing corrective actions.

———

PREPARED STATEMENT OF HON. JOHN ROTH, INSPECTOR GENERAL,
U.S. DEPARTMENT OF HOMELAND SECURITY

Chairman Fischer, Ranking Member Booker, and members of the Subcommittee, thank you for inviting me to testify at today's hearing regarding the security of our surface transportation infrastructure.

When the American public thinks of TSA, they think of the Transportation Security Officer in a blue shirt instructing them to remove their belts and shoes before going through security screening at the airport. The truth is that TSA has a much broader responsibility to also oversee and regulate our Nation's surface transportation modes—highway, freight and passenger rail, mass transit, and pipelines—and port security, to ensure the freedom of movement for people and commerce. However, TSA's budget reflects the public perception of its mission, allocating most of its resources to air passenger screening and dedicating only a small portion to the vulnerable areas of non-aviation.

Recently, the OIG has published three reports [1] that identify significant weaknesses in TSA's ability to secure surface transportation modes and the Nation's maritime facilities and vessels. Specifically, we identified issues with TSA's ability to identify risk across all modes of transportation, the reliability of background checks for port workers, and passenger rail security.

TSA Needs a Crosscutting Risk-Based Security Strategy

TSA has many responsibilities beyond air travel, and is responsible, generally through the use of regulation and oversight, for surface transportation security. However, TSA focuses primarily on air transportation security and largely ignores other modes. We found that TSA does not have an intelligence-driven, risk-based security strategy to inform security and budget needs across all types of transportation. In 2011, TSA began publicizing that it uses an "intelligence-driven, risk-based approach" across all transportation modes. However, we found this not to be true. In an audit we released this past September, we reported that TSA specifically designed this approach to replace its one-size-fits-all approach to air passenger screening but did not apply it to other transportation modes. Additionally, TSA's agency-wide risk management organizations provide little oversight of TSA's surface transportation security programs. TSA established an Executive Risk Steering Committee which was intended to create a crosscutting, risk-based strategy, which would drive resource allocations across all modes. However, neither it, nor any of these entities place much emphasis on non-air transportation modes.

We also found that TSA lacked a formal process to incorporate risk into its budget formulation decisions. Despite the disparate requirements on the agency, TSA dedicated 80 percent of its nearly $7.4 billion FY 2015 budget to direct aviation security expenditures, and only about 2 percent to direct surface transportation expenditures. Its remaining resources were spent on support and intelligence functions. A formal process that incorporates risk into its budget formulation would help TSA ensure it best determines and prioritizes the resources necessary to fulfill its missions.

TSA concurred with our recommendations, and is working to create a consolidated risk-based security strategy for aviation and surface transportation modes. It also noted that efforts were made to improve the budget process by conducting a series of crosscutting program reviews and developing resource planning guidance. However, notwithstanding that they have been working on this for a considerable amount of time, TSA does not intend to provide us with its risk-based security strategy until the last quarter of 2017. We also do not yet have their formal budget planning process that uses risk to inform resource allocations.

TSA Missing Key Controls within the TWIC Background Check Process

TSA—responsible for safeguarding our Nation's ports and maritime facilities through the Transportation Worker Identification Credential (TWIC) program—

---

[1] *TSA Oversight of National Passenger Rail System Security* (OIG–16–91); *TWIC Background Checks are Not as Reliable as They Could Be* (OIG–16–128); and *Transportation Security Administration Needs a Crosscutting Risk-Based Security Strategy* (OIG–16–134).

lacks key internal controls and this compromises the TWIC program's reliability. These weaknesses leave our Nation's seaports at risk for terrorist exploitation, smuggling, insider threats, and internal conspiracies.

TSA provides background checks, or security threat assessments, for individuals who need unescorted access to secure port facilities; and issues a biometric identification card, also known as a TWIC. The background check process for TWICs is the same as that of aviation workers [2] and drivers who need a Hazmat Materials Endorsement.[3] It includes a check for immigration-, criminal-, and terrorism-related offenses that would preclude someone from being granted unescorted access to secure facilities at seaports.

The Government Accountability Office (GAO) also reviewed the TWIC program five years ago. In 2011, GAO identified key internal control weaknesses in TSA's management of the TWIC background check process and recommended the Department take significant steps to improve the effectiveness of the program as a whole. Although TSA took some steps to address GAO's concerns, our review—five years later—found that TSA did not adequately integrate the security measures intended to identify fraudulent applications into the background check process.

For example, TSA required enrollment staff to use a digital scanner that could evaluate security features present on identification documents and generate a score to help TSA determine if the document was authentic. However, TSA did not collect or use these scores when completing its background checks—nullifying the effectiveness of this security measure. For those documents that could not be electronically scanned, TSA required the staff at the enrollment centers to manually review identity documents. However, TSA did not require that the staff be trained at detecting fraudulent documents. When the enrollment staff documented their observations of suspicious identity documents in TSA's system, TSA did not have a standardized process for collecting, reviewing, or using the notes when completing the background checks.

We determined TSA management's lack of oversight was the primary reason the TWIC background check process had many control weaknesses. At the time of our review, the TWIC background check process was divided among multiple program offices so that no single entity had complete oversight and authority over the program. Furthermore, the lead program office for the program lacked key metrics to measure TSA's success in achieving TWIC program core objectives. For example, the measures in place focused on customer service, such as enrollment time and help desk response time, rather than on areas like accuracy of the background check itself. Since our review, TSA told us it realigned the divisions responsible for the TWIC background check process in an effort to provide better oversight and guidance and has begun making improvement to strengthen the controls surrounding the background check process. However, we have not validated the TSA's actions, so we do not know whether this has improved the program's functionality.

TSA Delays Implementing Passenger Rail Security Regulations

TSA has failed to develop and implement regulations governing passenger rail security required more than nine years ago by the *Implementing Recommendations of the 9/11 Commission Act of 2007 (9/11 Act).*[4] Unlike the security presence that TSA provides air passengers in airports, its responsibility for rail passengers rests in assessing intelligence, sharing threat information with industry stakeholders, developing industry best practices, and enforcing regulations. This is particularly important due to the volume of passengers using this mode of transportation and the unique challenges in the rail environment.

In Fiscal Year 2015 alone, Amtrak carried 31 million passengers across the continental United States and Canada, and operated more than 300 trains daily. Additionally, Amtrak and other passenger rail carriers operate in an open infrastructure with multiple access points that make it impractical to subject all rail passengers to the type of security screening that passengers undergo at airports. Notwithstanding this, there were actions that TSA could have taken, but did not, that would have strengthened rail security. Specifically, although required to by the *9/11 Act,* TSA neither identified high-risk carriers nor issued regulations requiring those carriers to conduct vulnerability assessments and implement DHS-approved security plans. TSA also did not issue regulations that would require a railroad security training program and security background checks for frontline employees. Regula-

---

[2] *TSA Can Improve Aviation Worker Vetting* (OIG–15–98)

[3] Commercial drivers required to transport hazardous materials must undergo a background check by TSA prior to receiving a hazardous material endorsement on their Commercial Driver's License.

[4] Public Law 110–53.

tions to implement a training program are important to ensure rail carriers have a mechanism in place to prepare rail employees for potential security threats.

Furthermore, unlike aviation and maritime port workers, TSA did not develop regulations requiring security background checks for rail workers. TSA vets airport and maritime port workers who need unescorted access to secure areas against the terrorist watchlist and immigration status and criminal history information, and these processes are consistent with the requirements in the *9/11 Act*.

These very issues were identified in 2009 by GAO, which reported that TSA had only completed one of the key passenger rail requirements from the *9/11 Act*. Seven years later, we identified that the same rail requirements—a regulation for rail carriers to complete security assessments, a regulation for rail security training, and a program for conducting background checks on rail employees—remain incomplete.

Following the 2004 terrorist attack on a passenger train in Madrid, Spain, TSA issued a security directive for Amtrak. That directive required carriers to improve security procedures by designating a rail security coordinator, reporting significant security concerns to TSA, and allowing TSA to conduct inspections for any potential security threats. TSA does conduct some limited inspections to verify carrier compliance with these requirements. However, TSA does not enforce other aspects of the security directive, such as the use of bomb-resistant trash receptacles, canine teams, rail car inspections, and passenger identification checks to enhance security and deter terrorist attacks. Instead, TSA relies on Amtrak and other transit entities to implement security measures if resources permit, and is even considering rescinding these minimal requirements from the directive. Without enforcing all security requirements, TSA diminishes the directives importance and carriers ability to prevent or deter acts of terrorism.

In the absence of issuing formal regulations to implement the *9/11 Act* requirements, TSA has developed and implemented a variety of outreach programs and voluntary initiatives to strengthen rail security for Amtrak. However, Amtrak is not required to participate or implement TSA's recommended security measures because the initiatives are voluntary. TSA's reliance on voluntary initiatives has created an environment of reduced urgency to implement regulations governing passenger rail security; to establish a rail training program; and to conduct security background checks of frontline rail employees. If TSA does not fulfill these requirements, it cannot ensure that passenger rail carriers will implement security measures that may prevent or deter acts of terrorism.

Pending Legislation

Many of the issues I've discussed today are addressed in the *Surface Transportation and Maritime Security Act*. I want to thank the Committee for introducing legislation to address a number of the challenges facing the Department. We believe that if enacted, this legislation will direct numerous improvements to our Nation's security. However, I must emphasize that the Department and TSA have demonstrated a pattern of being dismissive and lax on implementing requirements related to non-aviation security, as illustrated in the attached appendix. Under these circumstances, change will require significant attention by Congress, the Inspector General, and the Comptroller General to ensure that TSA and the Department take timely actions to implement these improvements.

Future work

We will continue to audit and evaluate the Department's aviation and non-aviation-related programs and report our results. Currently, we are reviewing the effectiveness of TSA checkpoint screening, Federal Air Marshal oversight of civil aviation, the TSA PreCheck enrollment process, the TSA's Office of Intelligence and Analysis, and TSA's use of the Sensitive Security Information designation. We are planning a review of passenger security for cruise ships.

Madame Chairman, this concludes my testimony. I welcome any questions you or any other members of the Subcommittee may have.

OFFICE OF INSPECTOR GENERAL
Department of Homeland Security

Appendix

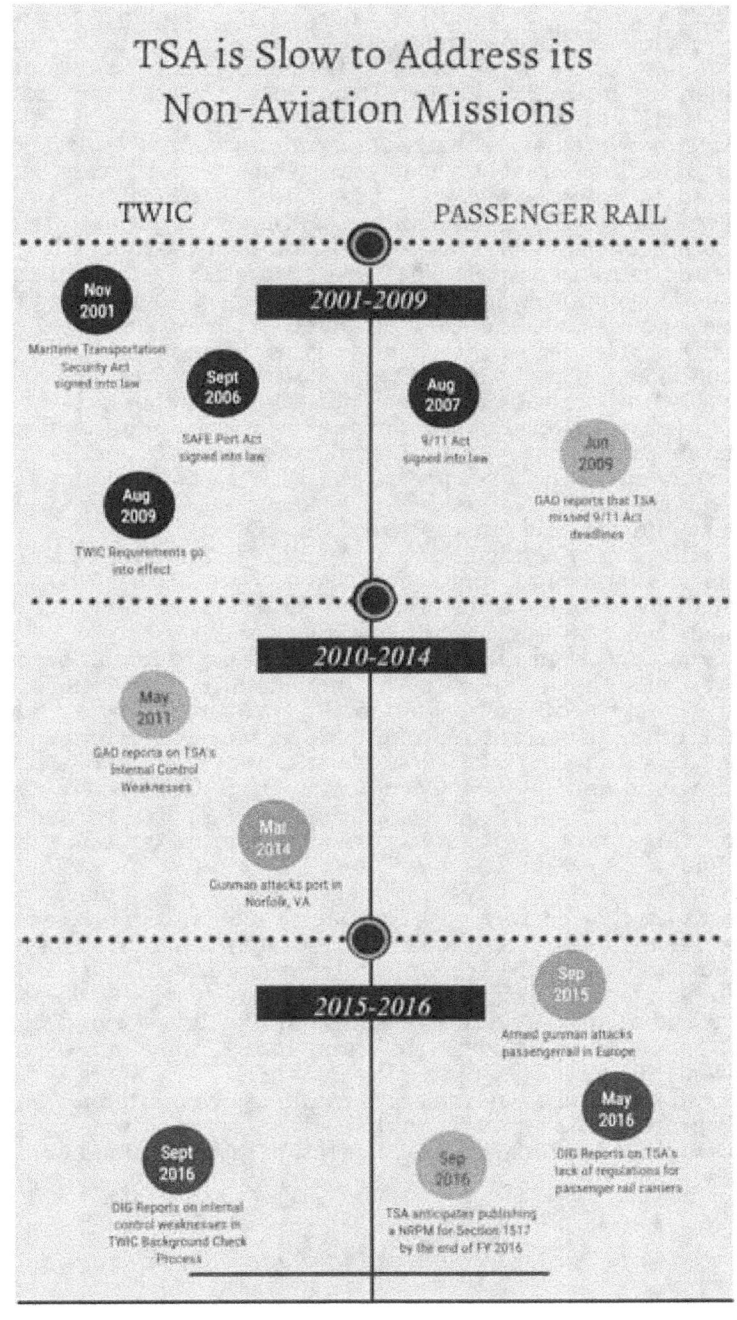

Senator FISCHER. Thank you very much.

Next, we have Chief Neil Trugman, who is the Interim Chief of Police at Amtrak.

Welcome.

STATEMENT OF NEIL TRUGMAN, INTERIM CHIEF OF POLICE, AMTRAK

Mr. TRUGMAN. Good afternoon, Madam Chair, Senator Booker, and members of the Committee. Thank you very much for the invitation to speak today. Amtrak takes its responsibility to protect its passengers, employees, and patrons seriously. And on behalf of Amtrak's new CEO, Mr. Charles "WICK" Moorman, and the men and women of the Amtrak Police Department, I am happy to discuss our efforts with you.

Amtrak serves more than 500 communities in 46 states, carrying over 31 million travelers last year, which was a record. APD was created to protect employees, passengers, stations, and critical infrastructure. Uniform officers are the most visible patrol presence, performing right-of-way inspections, random passenger bag screening, and regular patrols. They are supported by the Special Operations Division that specializes in counterterrorism, countersurveillance, and response tactics to include K–9 operations.

APD is a leader in the vapor wake K–9 program, which is capable of detecting explosive particles in the air as someone passes by. Our K–9 program of both conventional and vapor wake detection dogs averages over 1,000 train rides a month. Additionally, we coordinate with numerous local, state, and Federal agencies, and Amtrak detectives are assigned to the FBI, National Joint Terrorism Task Force at the National Counterterrorism Center, as well as the JTTFs and key field officers across the country.

We have also trained Amtrak employees and passengers to spot suspicious behaviors and report the activity to the APD by phone or text. The ability to leverage our skilled workforce and our passengers contributes greatly to our safety and security.

We have worked diligently in recent years to install security improvements that align with the implementing regulations of the 9/11 Commission Act, Section 1513(b), which authorizes Amtrak to allocate its DHS grant funding to 22 permissible counter-terrorism purposes. And Amtrak has undertaken numerous initiatives, including adding K–9 teams; conducting DHS ISTEP exercises, which are the Intermodal Security Training and Exercise Program; and improving station security, surveillance, and station hardening measures.

While some formal regulations are under development, Amtrak has worked to comply with the spirit and affordable security requirements of the Act, including security planning, risk assessments, and employee training. Furthermore, we have received the Gold Standard ranking from TSA after last year's baseline assessment and security evaluation. This is TSA's highest ranking.

Over the years, Federal investment to implement security improvements aimed at protecting Amtrak's passengers, employees, and infrastructure has varied. Amtrak receives Intercity Passenger Rail grant funds through annual DHS appropriations for security projects that are linked to transportation security fundamentals as described in grant funding guidance and are consistent with Section 1513 of the 9/11 Act. These areas generally fall into programs associated with security best practices: planning and assessments; infrastructure protection; security awareness, training, and exercises; and operational packages and equipment.

In 2008 and 2009, Amtrak received over $25 million from the Intercity Passenger Rail grant program, but since 2012, appropriations have dropped to $10 million. At this level, the ability of Amtrak to reduce risk and protect passengers is reduced.

With sufficient funding, Amtrak could implement a wide range of identified risk management solutions for infrastructure protection, such as expanded video surveillance, next-generation access control systems, and more high-security fencing. The APD would be able to expand its K–9 program, deploy additional security services, and increase the number of screening teams nationally. These improvements would greatly benefit the traveling public and ensure the Nation's investment in Amtrak receives the protection it deserves.

I look forward to answering any questions you might have about Amtrak's transportation security program.

Thank you.

[The prepared statement of Mr. Trugman follows:]

PREPARED STATEMENT OF NEIL TRUGMAN, INTERIM CHIEF OF POLICE, AMTRAK

Good morning Madam Chair, Senator Booker and members of the Committee. Thank you very much for the invitation to speak today. Amtrak takes its responsibility to protect its passengers, employees and patrons seriously, and on behalf of Amtrak's new CEO, Mr. Charles "WICK" Moorman, and the men and women of the Amtrak Police Department (APD), I'm happy to discuss these issues with you.

Amtrak serves more than 500 communities in 46 states, carrying over 31 million travelers last year, a record, and we have carried more than thirty million riders for the last six years. APD was created to protect employees, passengers, stations, rolling stock and critical infrastructure. Uniformed officers are the most visible patrol presence, supported by a Special Operations Division that receives special training in prevention, detection and response tactics. APD was a leader in "vapor wake" K–9 program, which are capable of detecting explosive particles in the air after someone carrying them has passed. APD performs counter-terrorism and counter-surveillance operations, random passenger bag screening, and right-of-way patrols. Our K–9 program of both conventional and vapor wake detection dogs averages 1,000 train rides a month. We coordinate with numerous other local, state, and Federal agencies, and Amtrak officers are assigned to the FBI National Joint Terrorism Task Force at the National Counter-Terrorism Center, as well as Joint Terrorism Task forces, in key field offices across the country.

Passenger rail security differs fundamentally from aviation security. Many railroad stations are a part of the urban fabric of city centers. The largest stations are multi-modal, hosting busses, subways and commuter rail with offices, food courts and retail establishments. New York Penn Station hosts more rail travelers annually than the La Guardia, JFK, and Newark Airports together. Daily commuting cycles require a fundamentally different security solution than airports, because urban terrain is different, and rail journeys are an organic part of our travelers' daily schedule.

Conversely, small rural stations are frequently unstaffed and provide access and connectivity between the Nation's heartland and its cities through an intercity route system. Screening every passenger prior to boarding in the passenger rail environment, as the airports do, is not feasible without resources and technology railroads don't currently possess. We do however, employ a variety of tactics to surveil key infrastructure and stations, while retaining robust capability to surge resources and leverage partnerships in unpredictable ways to complicate the task for an attacker. We coordinate with other law enforcement agencies and the intelligence community to respond to threats and adapt tactics in anticipation of potential new threats. We have also trained Amtrak's employees and passengers to spot and report suspicious behaviors including by phone or text. The ability to leverage our skilled workforce and our passengers contributes significantly to our safety and security.

We have also worked diligently in recent years to install security improvements that align with the Implementing Regulations of the 9/11 Commission Act. Section 1513(b) authorizes Amtrak to allocate its DHS grant funding to 22 permissible counterterrorism purposes, and Amtrak has undertaken numerous initiatives, including adding K–9 teams, conducting DHS-approved (Intermodal Security Training and Exercise Program), ISTEP exercises, improving station security and surveillance and station hardening measures. While some formal regulations are under development, Amtrak has worked to comply with the spirit and affordable security requirements of the Act, including security planning, risk assessments and employee training. Furthermore, we have received a "Gold" standard ranking from TSA after last year's Baseline Assessment and Security Evaluation. This is TSA's highest ranking.

Over the years, Federal investment to implement security improvements aimed at protecting Amtrak passengers, employees, and infrastructure has varied. Amtrak receives Intercity Passenger Rail (IPR) grant funds through annual DHS appropriations for security projects that are linked to transportation security fundamentals as described in grant funding guidance, and are consistent with Section 1513 of the 9/11 Act. These areas generally fall into programs associated with security best practices: planning and assessments; infrastructure protection; security awareness, training and exercises; and operational packages and equipment. In 2008 and 2009, Amtrak received over $25 million from the Intercity Passenger Rail grant program, but since 2012, appropriations have dropped to the $10 million level.

At this level, the ability of Amtrak to reduce risk and protect passengers is reduced. With sufficient funding, Amtrak could implement a wide range of identified risk management solutions for infrastructure protection, such as expanded video surveillance, next generation access control systems, and more high security fencing. The APD would be able to expand its K–9 program, deploy additional security services and increase the number of screening teams nationally. These improvements would greatly benefit the traveling public and ensure the Nation's investment in Amtrak receives the protection it deserves.

I look forward to answering any question you might have about Amtrak's transportation security program.

Senator FISCHER. Thank you very much.

Next, we have Mr. Chris Spear, who is the President and CEO of the American Trucking Association.

Welcome.

STATEMENT OF CHRIS SPEAR, PRESIDENT AND CEO, AMERICAN TRUCKING ASSOCIATION (ATA)

Mr. SPEAR. Thank you, Chairman Fischer, Ranking Member Booker, and distinguished members of the Subcommittee. Thank you for the opportunity to testify today. My name is Chris Spear. I am the President and CEO of the American Trucking Association, with a membership through our affiliated partners of more than 30,000 companies and every type and class of motor carrier operation.

The trucking industry is an integral component of our nation's economy, transporting more than 80 percent of our nation's freight and employing approximately 7 million workers in trucking related jobs, including over 3.5 million commercial drivers. It's also important to note that the trucking industry is comprised primarily of small businesses, with 97.3 percent of trucking companies operating 20 trucks or less and 90.8 percent operating six trucks or less. Most importantly, the trucking industry now spends more than $9.5 billion each year on safety enhancements to help ensure that drivers and passengers of all vehicles make it safely to their destination.

ATA also places great emphasis on security, the topic of today's hearing. Our focus is on strengthening transportation security without undermining economic security. To do this, we must rationalize the various credential requirements commercial drivers use, whether it be one federally issued credential or a credential with a Federal background check, such as a hazardous materials endorsement, to satisfy any Federal regulation that requires having a criminal history records check to operate in a facility or to conduct certain operations.

Having drivers undergo multiple, duplicative screenings, in our view, undermines our Nation's economic security by posing a direct financial burden on drivers and motor carriers and further depleting scarce Federal Government resources. Since MTSA authorized TWIC in 2002, ATA has advocated a one credential or screening, many-uses policy to balance the flow of commerce without compromising the security of our Nation's supply chain.

ATA strongly believes that the TWIC can serve as a universal credentialing background check, as well as a physical access control security mechanism at regulated port facilities. If the role of TWIC is to prevent acts of terror from occurring and to stop possible terrorists from obtaining access to secure areas of MTSA regulated facilities, one could argue this objective is being met. Yet the timeline for achieving this goal is unsatisfactory at best.

Redundancy of security threat assessments has still not been addressed. It has been 15 years since the tragic events of September 11, yet commercial drivers are still required to get a background check for TWIC, HME, and Free and Secure Trade, as well as different airport checks. Imagine requiring two separate cards for getting to and from the House and Senate. That's just two locations. Now multiply that number by the thousands, and we begin to understand what commercial drivers and carriers face every day.

Adopting a one credential or screening, many-uses policy would fix this problem. Absent this policy, ATA's highest security priority will continue to be the multiplicity of background checks and their associated costs and burdens. Drivers must undergo these checks to perform their everyday work responsibilities, including transporting hazardous materials, delivering at maritime facilities, crossing international borders, and transporting air cargo.

ATA has consistently supported a system and process that provides for a criminal history records check through national data bases. Today's threats aren't against one or more states, but America itself. In my previous life, I worked in the Middle East; North Africa; Central Asia, including Iraq, Syria, and Libya, and I've encountered elements that hold America in disdain. They don't chant "death to Nebraska" or New Jersey. They chant "death to the United States."

So if we're serious about protecting our homeland, then we must eliminate reactive behavior that results in redundant policies and practices. This is why the ATA supports the TWIC as the potential single credential and Security Threat Assessment that, in turn, can demonstrate and provide compliance with multiple programs and regulations.

TSA has not yet provided for full recognition of one STA for compliance with another regulatory STA, for instance, permitting

TWIC holders seeking an HME to follow their TWIC as proof of already having an equivalent STA. This is a policy that is supported statutorily by Section 1556 of the 9/11 Commission Act, whereas other Federal agencies, including DOD, are accepting the TWIC for compliance with their credentialing requirements.

ATA continues to voice its concern with GAO's suggestion that Congress consider alternative credentialing approaches which might include a more decentralized approach for achieving TWIC program goals. A decentralized approach is inherently flawed, will elevate security risks, inflict harm to our economy, and further delay adoption of a one credential or screening, multiple-use policy.

ATA supports the DHS serving as the primary authority in coordinating and managing security programs affecting the transportation sector. In that vein, harmonizing the consolidation of the motor carrier requirements pertaining to security background checks, security plans, security training, and corporate security reviews is and remains an elevated industry priority.

ATA also supports the Surface Transportation and Maritime Security Act, S. 3379, recently introduced by this committee, which would take steps to reduce costly and unnecessary background check requirements on drivers, specifically by allowing TWIC holders to obtain their hazmat endorsement without the need for additional background checks.

A secondary security priority for the ATA is also cybersecurity. This is an issue that we are very keen to address, as it becomes more applicable to an integrated trucking industry, and a topic that I would be more than eager to take questions on today.

Protecting our Nation's critical infrastructure is a key priority for the trucking industry, as it is essential to our Nation's security and economic prosperity. Threats to our Nation's roadways pose a danger to the motoring public and the security of our complex supply chain. The ATA stands ready to support Congress and DHS to be sure that enhanced national security and the unencumbered flow of commerce remain compatible priorities.

Thank you.

[The prepared statement of Mr. Spear follows:]

PREPARED STATEMENT OF CHRIS SPEAR, PRESIDENT AND CEO, AMERICAN TRUCKING ASSOCIATIONS (ATA)

Introduction

Chairman Fischer, Ranking Member Booker and distinguished members of the subcommittee, thank you for the opportunity to testify today on "Assessing the Security of our Critical Surface Transportation Infrastructure." My name is Chris Spear, and I am the President and CEO of the American Trucking Associations (ATA). Founded in 1933, ATA is the Nation's preeminent organization representing the interests of the U.S. trucking industry. Directly and through its affiliated organizations, ATA encompasses more than 30,000 companies and every type and class of motor carrier operation.

The trucking industry is an integral component of our Nation's economy, transporting more than 80 percent of our Nation's freight and employing approximately 7 million workers in trucking-related jobs, including over 3.5 million commercial drivers.[1] It is also important to note that the trucking industry is comprised primarily of small businesses, with 97.3 percent of trucking companies operating 20 trucks or less, and 90.8 percent operating six trucks or less.[2] Approximately 80 per-

---

[1] American Trucking Associations, *American Trucking Trends 2016* (August 2016)
[2] American Trucking Associations, *American Trucking Trends 2016* (August 2016).

cent of all U.S. communities depend solely on trucks to deliver and supply their essential commodities.[3] Most importantly, the trucking industry now spends more than $9.5 billion each year on safety enhancements to help ensure that drivers and passengers of all vehicles make it safely to their destination.[4]

ATA also places great emphasis on security. Our focus is on strengthening transportation security without undermining economic security. To do this, we must rationalize the various credential requirements commercial drivers use, whether it be one federally issued credential or a credential with a Federal background check, such as a Hazardous Materials Endorsement (HME), to satisfy any Federal regulation that requires a criminal history records check to operate in a facility or to conduct certain operations. Having drivers undergo multiple duplicative screenings undermines our Nation's economic security by posing a direct financial burden on drivers and motor carriers and further depleting scarce Federal Government resources. In short, this current and longstanding lack of coordination among Federal agencies in harmonizing or coordinating screening requirements is not a viable operating environment for motor carriers and commercial drivers.

The Problem with Alternative Credentialing Approaches

Since the Maritime Transportation Security Act (MTSA) of 2002 (Sec 102 of PL 107–295) authorized the Transportation Worker Identification Card (TWIC), ATA has advocated a "one credential or screening, many uses" policy to balance the flow of commerce without compromising the security of our Nation's supply chain. ATA strongly believes that the TWIC can serve as a universal credentialing/background check as well as a physical access control security mechanism at regulated port facilities. If the goal for TWIC is to prevent acts of terror from occurring and to stop possible terrorists from obtaining access to secure areas of MTSA-regulated facilities, one could argue that this objective is being met. Yet the timeline for achieving this goal is unsatisfactory at best. It has been 15 years since MTSA was enacted, 9 years since the TWIC final rule became effective, and still America has to wait two more years before TWIC readers are to be fully implemented. While one could argue that this is measurable progress, ATA believes that we can and must do better.

Redundancy of security threat assessments has still not been addressed. It has been 15 years since the tragic events of September 11, yet commercial drivers are still required to get a background check for TWIC, HME and Free and Secure Trade (FAST), as well as different checks for airports. Imagine requiring two separate cards for getting to and from the House and Senate. That's just two locations. Now multiply that number by the thousands and we begin to understand what commercial drivers and carriers face every day. Currently, there are 2.1 million active TWIC cards out of more than 3.5 million issued.[5] When dealing with over 700,000 drivers,[6] that have acquired the TWIC since 2007; requiring access to thousands of sensitive sites throughout the nation, the numbers tell the story.

The Solution is TWIC

Adopting a "one credential or screening, many uses" policy would fix this problem. Absent this policy, ATA's highest security priority will continue to be the multiplicity of background checks and their associated costs and burdens. Drivers must undergo these checks to perform their everyday work responsibilities, including transporting hazardous materials, delivering at maritime facilities, crossing international land borders and transporting air cargo. ATA has consistently supported a system and process that provides for a criminal history records check through national databases. Today's threats aren't against one or more states, but America itself. If we're serious about protecting our homeland, then we must eliminate reactive behavior that results in redundant policies and practices. This is why ATA supports the TWIC as the potential single credential and Security Threat Assessment (STA) that, in turn, can demonstrate and provide compliance with multiple programs and regulations.

---

[3] ATA staff, developed the 80 percent figure by using the Rand McNally Commercial & Marketing Guide (2001) numbers for rail service to communities and calculating the inverse, ultimately deriving the number of communities serviced by truck.

[4] American Trucking Associations, (2016, June 26). *Trucking Industry Spends $9.5 Billion In Safety Annually*. Retrieved from: *http://www.trucking.org/ATA%20Docs/News%20and%20Information/Reports%20Trends%20and%20Statistics/06%2028%2016%20%20Trucking%20Industry%20Invests%20$9%205%20Billion%20in%20Safety%20Annually.pdf*

[5] Office of Inspector General; Department of Homeland Security (2016). *TWIC Background Checks are Not as Reliable as They Could Be* (OIG–16–128)

[6] ATA staff was given this number by DHS, Office of Security Policy and Industry Management

TSA has not yet provided for full recognition of one STA for compliance with another regulatory STA, for instance permitting TWIC holders seeking an HME to show their TWIC as proof of already having an equivalent STA. This is a policy that is supported statutorily by Section 1556 of the 9/11 Commission Act, whereas other Federal agencies are accepting the TWIC for compliance with their credentialing requirements. For example, the Department of Defense (DOD) has established policy allowing commercial drivers transporting freight in and out of appropriate military facilities to use a TWIC in lieu of obtaining a DOD-issued Common Access Card (CAC). DOD acceptance of the TWIC for such purposes is recognition of the strength of the TWIC STA process and its compliance with Federal Personal Identity Verification (PIV) standards used by millions of Federal employees.

The Government Accountability Office (GAO) issued a report three years ago [7] criticizing TSA's planning shortfalls for implementing the TWIC reader pilot in a manner that did not yield usable information due to data-collection challenges. While ATA recognizes that TSA faced some technology challenges in collecting TWIC-reader functionality data, we would also point out that certain facilities using the TWIC readers successfully verified the credentials' status, identifying and improving throughput for truck operations. Additional focus should be given to facilities that have successfully implemented the TWIC readers, utilizing the "lessons-learned" and applying them to other facilities facing reader challenges.

ATA continues to voice its concern with GAO's suggestion that Congress consider "alternative credentialing approaches, which might include a more decentralized approach for achieving TWIC program goals." [8] A decentralized approach is inherently flawed, will elevate security risks, inflict harm to our economy and further delay adoption of a "one credential or screening, multiple uses" policy. Specifically, a decentralized approach would result in an environment in which each state or location performs STAs and issues separate credentials for truck drivers to access maritime facilities throughout the country. Such a scenario would result in an increasingly burdensome, inefficient and ineffective system for transportation workers who work and operate at multiple MTSA-regulated facilities. In contrast, the TWIC serves as a robust, nationwide, uniform STA that can be utilized at multiple locations when matched with the appropriate readers. For GAO to legitimately stand by its recommendation for decentralization, it would first need to explain why DOD's command and control administration of its CAC credential and the measurable benefits

it provides its holders around the world should do the same. Such a suggestion would be baseless, just as it is for the TWIC credential. The TSA and Coast Guard need to focus their efforts on ensuring the successful deployment of TWIC readers nationwide rather than creating a vast assortment of individual systems, which, unfortunately our Nation still has 16 years after TWIC was authorized by Congress.

ATA supports the implementation of the TWIC readers to improve security as well as throughput at maritime facilities for commercial vehicles. ATA asks Congress to remain vigilant during the implementation of the TWIC reader final rule; holding DHS accountable for ensuring that personnel working throughout our country's critical transportation infrastructure have been properly screened and continue to be vetted through relevant databases. Moreover, when the credential is utilized with the appropriate readers, it can ensure the validity of the card, match the TWIC to the cardholder, and allow for improved throughput when entering secure areas requiring these systems.

Some TWIC Progress Being Made

Setting the ATA's standing request for a "one credential or screening, many uses" policy aside, there are specific instances of progress with respect to TWIC that ATA can report to this subcommittee. In 2014, ATA submitted written testimony to the Senate Committee on Homeland Security and Governmental Affairs.[9] At that time, we provided an update on several challenges and opportunities facing the full adoption of TWIC based on day-to-day experiences of the trucking industry, including:

- The excessively high cost of the TWIC;
- The extended time the application process requires of applicants, taking time off work twice; once to apply and provide the biometrics; and, a second visit to pick up the credential;

---

[7] Government Accounting Office (2013), *Transportation Worker Identification Credential: Card Reader Pilot Results Are Unreliable; Security Benefits Should Be Reassessed,* (GAO–13–695T)

[8] Federal Government Approaches to Issuing Biometric IDs: Hearing before the Subcommittee on Government Operations of the Committee of Oversight and Government Reform, House of Representatives, 113th Congress (2013) (Testimony of Stephen M. Lord)

[9] Evaluating Port Security: Progress Made and Challenges Ahead: Hearing before the Committee on Homeland Security and Governmental Affairs, Senate (2014)

- The failure to expand TWIC's utilization to satisfy other Federal STA regulatory requirements, including identical STA programs within the Transportation Security Administration (TSA);
- The past lack of TWIC enrollment facilities nationwide to facilitate the enrollment of transportation workers who live far from either coast; and,
- The failure to implement the TWIC rule with its essential counterpart reader rule, annulling the credential's technology benefits and serving only as an expensive "flash-pass."

Since citing these five concerns in 2014, ATA is pleased to report that it has witnessed moderate improvements. The cost of the TWIC just two years ago was $129.50. It is now $125.25 for new applicants; $105.25 for new applicants with a valid HME; and, a replacement card is now $60.00. That said, the combined costs for TWIC and HME screenings have well surpassed $200 million, paid for entirely by the trucking industry as part of the overall cost to keep our Nation safe.

While the TSA website still cites an extended wait time of 4 to 6 weeks for applications to process, TWIC applications are now reportedly being processed in as little as two weeks. Applicants also don't have to take as much time off to acquire their actual credential. In July of 2014, TSA allowed for the "one visit" program to go national. The second visit to pick up a TWIC from the enrollment center was no longer required. Applicants could now have their TWIC or replacement TWIC mailed to their home.

The failure to expand the utilization of TWIC has also improved since 2014, but unfortunately not by much. Drivers with TWIC cards are deemed to have met the requirements for the Personnel Surety Program (PSP) under Chemical Facility Anti-Terrorism Standards of 2014 [10] and have the ability to use the TWIC to enter covered facilities and installations.

The lack of enrollment centers has been addressed by the contractor as suggested in our 2014 testimony. Forty-one states now use the universal enrollment for TSA and the fingerprint locations can also be kiosks at state DMV's.

As for implementation of the reader rule, the U.S. Coast Guard put out this rule in August of this year and it is currently expected to go into effect August 23, 2018. The rule, however, uses a tier level system, where only the highest level are required to use the readers. If that occurs, many of ATA's members required to have TWIC may not have their card scanned.

ATA members, specifically drivers and carriers, will continue to serve on the front line where they experience the successes and shortfalls of TWIC. That being the case, ATA will continue to update Congress as well as provide comments to DHS and its agencies on these and any other challenges that may arise to help improve the TWIC program and balance the importance of transportation and economic security.

ATA supports the DHS serving as the primary authority in coordinating and managing security programs affecting the transportation sector. In that vein, harmonization and consolidation of motor carrier requirements pertaining to security background checks, security plans, security training and corporate security reviews is and remains an elevated industry priority. ATA also supports the Surface Transportation and Maritime Security Act (S. 3379) recently introduced by the committee, which would take steps to reduce costly and unnecessary background check requirements on drivers, specifically by allowing TWIC holders to obtain their hazmat endorsement without the need for additional background checks. Such reforms will continue to improve the efficiency of goods movement without hindering our national security interests.

Cybersecurity

A secondary security priority for the ATA is the need to continue harmonizing any security requirement on carriers to harden their operations when transporting certain types of cargo or operating in environments that require a higher degree of security. Trucking is not exempt from the threats of cybersecurity. Our industry will continue to work with service providers as well as government agencies to improve our cybersecurity posture and make certain that our systems and protocols are never compromised.

The number of cyberattacks throughout the country continues to climb, compromising countless businesses and threatening consumer and personal privacy. Moving the majority of our Nation's freight and adopting more technology that our industry requires to remain competitive and efficient makes trucking equally suscep-

---

[10] Protecting and Securing Chemical Facilities from Terrorist Attacks Act of 2014, Pub. L. 113–254. § 2102, 128 Stat.2909 (2014)

tible to cyber threats. Trucking companies have already been victims of "ransomware" (*i.e.,* locked out of their servers with demands for money to resume access) and have had sensitive business information stolen.

In October, hackers initiated a denial of service attack that caused a massive Internet outage, leading to widespread disruption of commerce and usage among Americans who rely upon the Internet for a wide variety of transactions. The trucking industry is ever mindful of such threats, especially while the debate over autonomous vehicles unfolds. While the potential of automated trucks to improve highway safety and save lives is significant, so is the danger posed by cyber criminals and terrorists. ATA will continue to advocate for a policy framework on autonomous vehicles that will ensure public safety and reduce threats to our Nation's infrastructure, while also encouraging innovation in this rapidly changing environment where the benefits of improving safety, reducing emissions and fuel burn, eliminating congestion and increasing productivity may ultimately reside.

The ATA also supports voluntary supply chain security programs that embrace stakeholder input, adopting best practices established by industry, and offering motor carriers valuable benefits in exchange for program participation. The sharing of information is yet another key component of the private and public sectors working in partnership to implement coordinated and integrated protective security measures.

Conclusion

Protecting our Nation's critical transportation infrastructure is a key priority for the trucking industry, as it is essential to our Nation's security and economic prosperity. Threats to our Nation's roadways pose a danger to the motoring public and the security of our complex supply chain. The ATA remains committed to working with DHS to protect our highways from potential threats and mitigate the possibility of a truck conveyance from transporting or being used as a weapon. ATA has and will continue to actively participate as a member of the Highway and Motor Carrier Sector Coordinating Council to work with other industry stakeholders and our government partners to identify and implement solutions to improve the security of our Nation's critical surface transportation infrastructure. Regulation for the sake of regulation, however, is not a solution. Security regulations should continually seek to effectively balance national security interests without hindering the efficient movement of goods throughout our economy by placing undue burdens or costs on industry and subsequently, consumers. In doing so, our increasingly connected world and trucking industry requires a mindset where cyber threats to our Nation's infrastructure can be just as consequential to public safety and our economy as physical attacks. The ATA stands ready to support Congress and DHS to be sure that enhanced national security and the unencumbered flow of commerce remain compatible priorities.

Senator FISCHER. Thank you, Mr. Spear.

Next, we have Mr. Tony Straquadine—did I pronounce your name right?

Mr. STRAQUADINE. Yes, ma'am. That's correct.

Senator FISCHER.—who is Manager of Commercial and Government Affairs at Alliance Pipeline and a Representative of the Interstate Natural Gas Association of America.

Welcome.

STATEMENT OF ANTHONY STRAQUADINE, JR., MANAGER, COMMERCIAL, GOVERNMENT AFFAIRS AND MANAGING U.S. OFFICER, ALLIANCE PIPELINE INC.

Mr. STRAQUADINE. Good afternoon, Chairwoman Fischer, Ranking Member Booker, and members of the Subcommittee. My name is Tony Straquadine. I'm appearing before you today as a representative of Alliance Pipeline and as a member company of the Interstate Natural Gas Association of America, or INGAA.

Alliance Pipeline is a 2,400-mile integrated Canadian and U.S. natural gas transmission system pipeline, delivering rich natural gas from Western Canada and North Dakota's Bakken formation to the Chicago market. We've been in commercial service since December 2000 and deliver an average of 1.6 billion cubic feet of natural gas per day. Each and every day, our staff focuses on the safe and reliable transportation of natural gas for our shippers. The abundant and affordable energy we transport is used for heating homes, creating affordable electricity, and revitalizing American manufacturing.

My testimony today will address a voluntary cybersecurity architecture review recently completed by Alliance Pipeline with staff from TSA and FERC's Office of Energy Infrastructure Security. I'll also provide brief comments on Senate Bill 3379, Surface Transportation and Maritime Security Act.

In August 2016, Alliance met for a two-day, voluntary cybersecurity architecture review with members of FERC's Office of Energy Infrastructure Security and TSA's Office of Security Policy and Industry Engagement. This review was designed to be a collaborative, non-regulatory approach that promotes secure and resilient infrastructure through the sharing of information and best practices.

The goal of the review was to gain a comprehensive understanding of the entity's overall cybersecurity posture, to identify potential areas of concern, and to articulate actionable recommendations and observations that promote positive change in the security posture of the reviewed organization. This review encompassed all aspects of Alliance's information systems and networks, including our industrial control systems.

While this review was led by FERC's Office of Energy Infrastructure Security, TSA staff actively participated to better understand the risks and best practice recommendations in the cybersecurity areas related to natural gas pipelines. TSA acknowledged that they have much to learn, and Alliance Pipeline supports TSA's effort to build their competencies in this area. I would also like to acknowledge the FERC team for their efforts in leading this review.

The outcome of this review was well received by all parties, as Alliance Pipeline received over 60 best practice observations and recommendations. Alliance is working to implement many recommendations that have been prioritized to ensure ongoing safe and efficient cybersecurity operations. Alliance has also recommended that other pipelines in our industry sector consider participating in a similar cybersecurity architecture review.

Alliance Pipeline has reviewed S. 3379, and on behalf of INGAA, we support this legislation with the following comments. First, we support the creation of an advisory committee as proposed in Section 8 of this bill but suggest that the broad array of different transportation modes being represented under one committee might limit more sector-specific expertise and involvement in the Committee. We would suggest either formal or informal subcommittees focused on specific sectors, such as marine or pipelines, which would allow for greater involvement within that sector in the advisory committee decisionmaking process.

Second, we agree with the comments on the Transportation Worker Identification Credential Program improvements and oversights as contained in Section 17. We also support the mission of TSA in their oversight role and look forward to working with the agency as they add additional departmental resources to interface with the pipeline sector, specifically.

With respect to both cyber and physical infrastructure security in the pipeline sector, we'd like to note that the energy pipeline industry is experiencing greater numbers of threats from those who want to attack infrastructure as a way to make a political statement about the use of fossil fuels. These threats are potentially dangerous and disruptive, and we note that to date, there has been a reluctance to prosecute these perpetrators. This is creating an appearance of a risk-free environment for future attacks on pipelines. Attacks on pipeline infrastructure should be treated in a consistent manner, whether those attacks are coming from a foreign state or whether such attacks are coming from demonstrators bent on making a dramatic impact with the media.

In conclusion, Alliance Pipeline supports improving cybersecurity review capabilities of TSA as it relates to the natural gas transmission pipeline industry. We also broadly support S. 3379 with the above noted recommendations.

Madam Chair, thank you again for the opportunity to provide insight into Alliance Pipeline's focus on maintaining safe and reliable natural gas pipeline operations which results in the reliable delivery of energy to heat our homes, fuel our economy, and keep the lights on. I'd be happy to answer questions at the appropriate time.

[The prepared statement of Mr. Straquadine follows:]

PREPARED STATEMENT OF ANTHONY STRAQUADINE, JR., MANAGER, COMMERCIAL, GOVERNMENT AFFAIRS AND MANAGING U.S. OFFICER, ALLIANCE PIPELINE INC.

Good afternoon Chairman Fischer, Ranking Member Booker, and members of the Subcommittee. My name is Tony Straquadine, and I am the Manager, Commercial, Government Affairs and Managing U.S. Officer for Alliance Pipeline Inc. I am appearing before you today as a representative of Alliance Pipeline and as a member company representing the Interstate Natural Gas Association of America (INGAA). Alliance Pipeline consists of a 2,391-mile integrated Canadian and U.S. natural gas transmission pipeline system, delivering rich natural gas from the Western Canadian Sedimentary Basin and the Williston Basin to the Chicago market hub. The United States portion of the system consists of approximately 967 miles of infrastructure including the 80-mile Tioga Lateral in North Dakota. Alliance has been in commercial service since December 2000 and, through an innovative suite of customer-focused services, delivers an average of 1.6 billion standard cubic feet of natural gas per day. Each and every day, Alliance Pipeline staff focuses on the safe and reliable transportation of natural gas for our shippers; those who live and work near our system; and our employees. The abundant and affordable energy we transport is used for heating homes, creating affordable electricity, and revitalizing American manufacturing.

As authorized under the Natural Gas Act, Alliance Pipeline is an interstate natural gas pipeline certificated by the Federal Energy Regulatory Commission (FERC). Alliance is also subject to pipeline design and safety oversight by the Department of Transportation's Pipeline and Hazardous Materials Safety Administration (DOT–PHMSA). Natural gas pipelines also operate with the benefit of the guidance of the Department of Homeland Security's Transportation Security Administration (DHS–TSA). TSA's surface transportation pipeline program is designed to enhance the security preparedness of the Nation's natural gas pipeline systems and provide cyber risk management information to surface transportation operations, including the U.S. Computer Emergency Readiness Team (US–CERT).

My testimony today will address a voluntary Cybersecurity Architecture Review recently completed by Alliance Pipeline with staff from DHS–TSA and the FERC Office of Energy Infrastructure Security (OEIS) staff. I will also provide brief comment on S. 3379, the draft bill titled "Surface Transportation and Maritime Security Act."

Voluntary Cybersecurity Architecture Review

During August 2016, led by Alliance Pipeline's President and CEO, Mr. Terrance Kutryk and senior Information Services staff, Alliance met for a two-day voluntary Cyber Security Architecture Review (the Review) with members of the FERC OEIS and DHS–TSA's Office of Security Policy and Industry Engagement. This Review was designed to be a collaborative, non-regulatory approach that promotes secure and resilient infrastructure through the sharing of information and best practices. The goal of the Review was to gain a comprehensive understanding of an entity's overall cybersecurity posture, to identify potential areas of concern, and to articulate actionable recommendations and observations that promote positive change to the security posture of the reviewed organization.

This Review encompassed the business environment, governance, risk management, teams and programs, cybersecurity awareness and training, supply chain security, and all company networks, including but not limited to corporate and industrial control systems. While this review was led by OEIS staff, DHS–TSA staff actively participated to better understand the risks and best-practice recommendations in the cybersecurity areas related to natural gas pipeline transmission systems. DHS–TSA clearly acknowledged that they had much to learn in the cybersecurity realm. Alliance Pipeline supports DHS–TSA's efforts to build their competency in this area. I'd also like to acknowledge FERC's OEIS team for their efforts in leading this Review.

In advance of this Review, Alliance completed an assessment against the National Institute of Standards and Technology (NIST) Cybersecurity framework. This NIST framework was acknowledged by OEIS as best practice.

The outcome of this Review was well received by all parties participating, as Alliance Pipeline received numerous best practice recommendations offered by OEIS and DHS–TSA. Alliance is working to implement many recommendations that have been prioritized to ensure ongoing safe and efficient cybersecurity operations. Alliance has also recommended that other pipelines in our industry sector consider participating in a similar Cybersecurity Architecture Review.

Alliance Pipeline Comments on the Surface Transportation and Maritime Security Act

Alliance Pipeline has reviewed the Surface Transportation and Maritime Security Act (the Act) draft, dated September 21, 2016. On behalf of INGAA, we support the legislation and offer the following comments.

First, we support the creation of an advisory committee as proposed in Section 8, but suggest that the broad array of different transportation modes being represented under one committee might limit more sector-specific expertise and involvement in the committee. We would suggest either formal or informal subcommittees focused on specific sectors, such as marine or pipelines, which would allow for greater involvement within that sector in the advisory committee decision-making.

Second, we agree with the transportation worker identification credential improvements and oversight contained in Section 17.

We support the mission of TSA in their oversight role, but hope that more emphasis can be placed on having adequate departmental personnel in place to interface with the pipeline sector.

With respect to both cyber and physical infrastructure security in the pipeline sector, we want to note that the energy pipeline industry is experiencing greater numbers of threats from those who want to attack infrastructure as a way to make a political statement about the use of fossil fuels. These threats are disruptive and potentially dangerous, and we note that to date there has been a reluctance to prosecute the perpetrators. Our industry's concern is that this could create the appearance of a "risk-free" environment for future attacks on pipelines. Attacks on pipeline infrastructure should be treated in a consistent manner, whether such attacks come from foreign states or from domestic activists bent on doing something dramatic for media attention.

Conclusion

Both Alliance Pipeline and INGAA support improving the cybersecurity review capability of DHS–TSA as it relates to the natural gas transmission pipeline industry. We also broadly support the Surface Transportation and Maritime Security Act with the above noted recommended modifications.

Madam Chair, thank you again for the opportunity to provide insight into Alliance Pipeline's focus on maintaining safe and reliable natural gas pipeline operations, which results in the reliable delivery of energy to heat our homes, fuel our economy and help keep our lights on. I would be happy to answer questions at the appropriate time.

Senator FISCHER. Thank you very much.

Next, we have Mr. Tom Belfiore, the Chief Security Officer of the Port Authority of New York and New Jersey.

Welcome, sir.

STATEMENT OF TOM BELFIORE, CHIEF SECURITY OFFICER, PORT AUTHORITY OF NEW YORK AND NEW JERSEY

Mr. BELFIORE. Thank you so much. Good afternoon, Honorable Chair of the Subcommittee.

Senator FISCHER. Good afternoon.

Mr. BELFIORE. Thank you for this privilege today to speak about the Port Authority's role in securing our critical surface transportation assets.

The Port Authority of New York and New Jersey conceives, builds, operates, and maintains infrastructure critical to the New York-New Jersey region's transportation and trade network. The assets we protect include six airports, including JFK, Newark, and LaGuardia; two tunnels, the Holland and Lincoln Tunnels; four bridges, including the George Washington Bridge; the Port Authority bus terminal at 42nd Street and 8th Avenue in Manhattan; the PATH rail system which moves 265,000 passengers each weekday; the ports of New York and New Jersey; and, of course, the World Trade Center complex in lower Manhattan.

Recent domestic and international events prove to us that now, more than ever, we must be prepared to address ever-growing, ever-evolving, and more lethal threats. The transportation sector and critical infrastructure assets remain as the most attractive tar- gets of terrorist organizations and lone actors. Particularly acute are the Port Authority's assets, as we operate the Nation's largest airport system, the busiest bus terminal, the most traveled bridge in the nation, the East Coast's busiest ports, and secure the World Trade Center.

The Port Authority employs a risk-based, intelligence-driven, multi-layered security approach to protect these critical infrastructure assets and all those who depend on them. The layers in the methodology are: being intelligence-led; measuring risk through a layered assessment process; police prevention and interdiction methods; operational security measures that include contract security resources; the deployment of available and developing technologies; the use of engineered hardening solutions; the Office of Emergency Management to include response and recovery; strong Federal, State, and regional partnerships and relationships; and, of course, we measure our effectiveness, audit, and revise the program constantly.

Our policing strategy is intelligence-led, as the Port Authority Police Department has a presence in 28 Federal, State, and local law enforcement task forces that include the FBI Joint Terrorism Task Force in both the states of New York and New Jersey. We are confident that we are connected to receive important and actionable intelligence and information in a timely fashion that will help us protect these critical assets.

Our PAPD is a highly competent and professional police agency that maintains a 24/7 command presence at our transportation facilities and assets. Our policing methods include routine uniform patrols, high visibility emergency service unit patrols, the deployment of dedicated counter-terrorism teams, as well as the assignment of explosive detection K–9 units and radiation detection capabilities.

Our police presence is supplemented by a contract security guard force of over 1,000 unarmed security officers who are trained in behavioral recognition techniques and counter-terrorism awareness.

These security officers are posted at critical locations throughout our facilities and also staff multiple 24/7 security operation centers.

In addition to our human assets, we have made significant investments in our capital security projects as directed by our periodic program of risk assessments that inform our investments to further strengthen our facilities. Since 2001, the Port Authority has spent close to $9.9 billion on operational and capital security measures. This includes over $1.2 billion spent in asset hardening of critical infrastructure.

For example, at our bridge facilities, we have protected suspension and main cables. At our PATH rail transit facilities, we have hardened our tunnels and have implemented flood protection strategies. At our marine facilities, we have installed complex access control and CCTV systems. We also continue to partner with Federal agencies in piloting state-of-the-art radiation detection technologies. In the coming years, we plan to spend nearly another billion dollars to further protect these assets.

The use of technology is of paramount importance. In addition to our agency-wide surveillance system of more than 6,000 CCTV cameras, the Port Authority has invested in robust card access control and alarming systems; perimeter and laser intrusion detection systems; detection devices that help protect against chemical, biological, and radiological threats; a robust radio communication system that allows for interoperability with our mutual aid partners and first responders. The Port Authority operates a 24/7 cybersecurity operation center that can receive alerts from our cyber defense tools and respond to threats to our network and equipment.

The Port Authority has its own Office of Emergency Management that is vital to this multi-layered protection scheme. They lead our agency-wide business continuity program. They manage and administer agency-wide security grants. They also plan and execute agency-wide training and full scale exercises. These remarkable training initiatives involve both agency personnel and our regional first responders. To date, over 27,000 Port Authority staff and regional partners have been trained on such topics as active shooter response, PATH rail emergencies, incident command, terrorism attacks, and other hazards.

In order to maintain a prepared, unified, and accountable security operation, the Port Authority regularly measures, audits, and inspects programs and systems. These internal auditing programs allow us to proactively identify and mitigate issues and concerns before our adversaries can discover and exploit them. Furthermore, in an effort to ensure independent third party review, the Port Authority participates in the Department of Homeland Security Safety Act Program. Since 2011, we have received a number of Safety Act certifications and designations.

So how can the Federal Government help? First and foremost, we thank you so much for the help we have received. We cannot do it without you. The Port Authority keeps security as a top priority. A critical resource is the Federal Grant Program. This funding source is essential to help us continue to protect our facilities from these ever-changing and evolving threats.

A large source of funding comes from the Transit Security Grant Program. In 2016, the maximum amount of funding through this program was set at $87 million nationwide. Of course, an increase in funding would allow transit operators to pursue larger capital security projects. We are also very appreciative of the efforts under-way to extend grant duration periods from three to five years, which can allow us to complete larger and more complex security enhancements.

In closing, I would like to thank the members of this sub-committee and our congressional delegation for their dedicated, un-wavering, and continuing support that allows us to better serve our employees and customers and to better protect our regional critical transportation infrastructure and perhaps, most importantly, all those that depend upon it.

Thank you so much.

[The prepared statement of Mr. Belfiore follows:]

PREPARED STATEMENT OF THOMAS BELFIORE, CHIEF SECURITY OFFICER, THE PORT AUTHORITY OF NEW YORK AND NEW JERSEY

About the Port Authority

The Port Authority of New York & New Jersey conceives, builds, operates and maintains infrastructure critical to the New York/New Jersey region's transportation and trade network. These facilities include America's busiest airport system, including: John F. Kennedy International, LaGuardia, and Newark Liberty International airports, marine terminals and ports, the PATH rail transit system, six tunnels and bridges between New York and New Jersey, the Port Authority Bus Terminal in Manhattan, and the World Trade Center. For more than ninety years, the Port Authority has worked to improve the quality of life for the more than 18 million people who live and work in New York and New Jersey metropolitan region.

The Office of the Chief Security Officer

Created in 2012, the Office of the Chief Security Officer (OCSO) is a department within the Port Authority and is responsible for providing the highest quality public safety, facility security operations, security program management, emergency management, and airport rescue and firefighting training and services. Together, over 2,000 employees ensure the security and safe movement of the Port Authority's customers, partners, employees, and stakeholders every day.

I. Port Authority New York and New Jersey Transportation Assets

The Port Authority builds, operates, and maintains critical transportation and trade assets that fall under our five (5) lines of business:

- Aviation
- Rail
- Tunnels, Bridges and Terminals
- Ports
- Commercial Real Estate

Our aviation assets include six (6) airports: John F. Kennedy International Airport, LaGuardia Airport, Newark Liberty International Airport, Teterboro Airport and Stewart International Airport. In 2015, Port Authority airports moved an estimated 124 million passengers.

Our rail and surface transportation assets include the Trans-Hudson Rail System (PATH), George Washington Bridge, Bayonne Bridge, Goethals Bridge, Outerbridge Crossing, the Port Authority Bus Terminal, George Washington Bridge Bus Station, Journal Square Transportation Center, Holland Tunnel and Lincoln Tunnel. In 2015, the PATH system carried over 76.5 million passengers; an average of 265,000 passengers per day. Additionally, over 115 million vehicles travel over PA's bridges and Tunnels annually.

Port Authority also manages ports that transport vital cargo throughout the New York and New Jersey region. The Port of New York and New Jersey is the largest on the east coast and in 2015 moved over 3.6 million cargo containers.

The Port Authority also owns and manages the 16-acre World Trade Center site, home to the iconic One World Trade Center.

The transportation sector and critical infrastructure assets remain as the most attractive targets of terrorists' organizations and lone actors; particularly acute are the Port Authority of New York and New Jersey assets, as we operate the Nation's largest airport system, the busiest Bus Terminal and most traveled bridge (GWB) in the nation, and the east coast's busiest ports. Outlined below are the tools and strategies we deploy to ensure our assets and the people who rely on them are safe and secure.

II. Our Multi-Layered Approach to Securing Our Assets and Protecting the Public

The tragic events of September 11, 2001, remain the single most important turning point in the role of security within the Port Authority. Since that time, the Port Authority has spent close to $9.9 billion on operational and capital security measures. These expenditures were guided by a robust risk-based, intelligence-driven, multi-layered security approach to protect the Port Authority's customers, the general public, employees, and critical infrastructure by developing, implementing, and managing programs that preserve life and property, increase safety and security, and support the Agency's business objectives by strengthening our resilience and continuity of operations. With these measures in place—there is no single point of failure. Our multi-layered approach is explained in detail below.

Intelligence-Led

The Port Authority Police Department (PAPD) implements intelligence-led policing to ensure our resources are effectively deployed to prevent potential threats to our customers, employees, and facilities. The PAPD has presence in 28 Federal, state, and local law enforcement task forces, to include: the Federal Bureau of Investigation Joint Terrorism Task Force (FBI JTTF) in New York and New Jersey which allows for shared intelligence across many agencies; the New York and New Jersey High-Intensity Drug Trafficking Areas (HIDTA) taskforce and the New Jersey State Police Regional Operations Intelligence Center (ROIC) that allows for the immediate exchange of important, timely and actionable intelligence for both sides of the Hudson.

Additionally, we have a stakeholder representative assigned fulltime to the New York Police Department's Lower Manhattan Security Initiative. This unit is a key provider of day-to-day actionable intelligence relative to routine conditions like large events and demonstrations to current and emerging threats.

These combined resources result in the agile, flexible, effective and efficient deployment of security and law enforcement resources that are responsive to current and developing threats and conditions.

Risk Assessments

As the owner and operator of multi-modal transportation assets, it is critical that the allocation of human and financial resources across our various facilities be determined using a risk-based approach. To that end, all-hazards risk assessments are performed on a regular basis to better understand changes in threats and vulnerabilities related to our facilities. Our periodic multi-hazard assessments look across all Agency assets and prioritize our risk to inform security and resource decisions across all of our transportation assets.

Police Interdiction Activities

The PAPD is comprised of over 1,900 uniformed police officers operating across thirteen (13) Port Authority facilities. The department also includes a Criminal Investigations Bureau, Special Operations Division, which includes an Emergency Services Unit and a Canine Unit (K–9), and an Aircraft Rescue and Firefighting component at the Port Authority airports.

Through visible uniformed police presence and in partnership with other law enforcement agencies, the PAPD suppresses crime and utilizes counterterrorism measures to thwart potential adversaries seeking to cause harm or disruption by way of an attack. PAPD also deploys high visibility patrols and specialized services to enhance basic patrol functions utilizing intelligence-led policing concepts.

Operational Security Measures and Security Agents

The Port Authority implements civilian security programs to supplement our police department activities and increase the levels of protection at our facilities. These programs safeguard Port Authority facilities from threats to physical infrastructure, unauthorized access to restricted areas, cybersecurity attacks, and breaches of protected security information.

Security policies, procedures, and operating protocols are ingrained at each of our facilities. A foundational element of protecting our facilities is granting access to certain secure areas only to authorized persons, after extensive criminal history checks are conducted. At our airports, the Federal Secure Identification Display Area (SIDA) program is utilized. For our maritime facilities, the Federal TWIC program is in effect and we support efforts to make this program as robust and reliable as possible.

We carry this model beyond where federally regulated to our other surface transportation facilities including tunnels, bridges, terminals, and rail facilities by requiring all third-party contractors and service vendors to undergo criminal history checks as well.

Additionally, the Port Authority employs over 1,000 unarmed Uniformed Contract Security Agents to guard our facilities and keep our employees and customers safe.

Technology

A critical element of a robust multi-layered approach is the development and maintenance of advanced technology systems to support both security and resiliency. Significant investments have been made in this area.

We employ an agency-wide video surveillance system of more than 6,000 Closed Circuit Television (CCTV) cameras with recording capabilities. Access control systems and alarming is in use at each of our facilities.

Perimeter intrusion detection systems are deployed at our airports and a laser intrusion detection system is in use at PATH to detect intrusions into our under-river tunnels from the track area.

Sensors and detection devices are in place in certain locations to help protect against chemical, biological and radiological threats.

With regard to radio communications, the Port Authority has invested over $110 million to deploy an agency-wide Police intra-operable 800 MHz radio system at all its facilities, enabling PAPD officers responding to an incident from a neighboring command (*e.g.,* Holland Tunnel, Newark Airport, etc.) to talk seamlessly with other PAPD officers assigned to a different command. Further, we have deployed antenna networks carrying National Mutual Aid channels in both the UHF and 800 MHz bands ("UTAC and 8TAC") into the PATH underground to assure radio inter-operability with our mutual aid partners, such as NYPD, FDNY, and the City of Jersey City first responder agencies.

Lastly, we have created a new Cyber Security program to better monitor and respond to suspicious activities occurring on our network, therefore strengthening our capability to protect our critical information and industrial control systems. The Port Authority operates a 24/7 cybersecurity operations center that can receive alerts from our cyber defense tools and respond to threats to our network and equipment.

Engineered Hardening Solutions

Since September 11, 2001, the Port Authority has made over $1.3 billion in asset hardening investments. Although faced with the challenge of retrofitting security features into existing facilities, we have implemented a multitude of hardening solutions. At our aviation facilities, we have placed bollards at all terminal frontages, enhanced perimeter fencing, strengthened vehicular guard posts, and are protecting terminal glass.

At our bridge facilities, we have protected suspension and main cables, strengthened the supporting towers, and created standoff to the bridge bases and piers from water-borne threats.

At our PATH rail transit facilities, we have installed tunnel hardening and flood mitigation strategies, while also protecting key rail support facilities with bollards, cameras, and access control.

At our maritime facilities, we have installed access control and CCTV systems, systems to allow for Port-wide emergency notifications, and enhancements to aid in evacuation of the Port. We continue to partner with Federal agencies in the piloting of state-of-the-art radiation detection technologies.

Office of Emergency Management

The Port Authority enhances resiliency, response, and recovery through our Office of Emergency Management (OEM). The OEM champions programs that provide the Port Authority with the resources, support, and capabilities to prepare for, respond to, recover from, and mitigate against all-hazards. The OEM is organized into three core mission areas:

Emergency Management. Supports the Incident Command response structure at Port Authority during events or incidents. Additionally, responsible for all-hazard planning and training for agency personnel and regional partners who will support our response activities to emergencies at our facilities located in New York and New Jersey. Through the use of tabletop and full-scale exercise, over 27,000 Port Authority staff and regional partners have been trained on such topics as Active Shooter response, PATH rail emergencies, terror attacks and other hazards.

Grant Management. Administers and manages all Federal and State Homeland Security Grants that allows us to harden our assets, invest in technology, initiate new programs, and provide for enhanced police protective services.

Risk Management and Resiliency. Responsible for coordinating and implementing the agency-wide all-hazard risk assessment and oversees the Port Authority Business Continuity program.

These programs are regularly adapted to meet the needs of the Port Authority with an impact range that stretches from individual employee preparedness to agency-wide, corporate-level resiliency.

Federal, State, and Regional Partnerships

The Port Authority understands the importance of maintaining strong relationships with our Federal, State and local partners. These cooperative partnerships are integral to our intelligence, counterterrorism, cybersecurity, technology, and training efforts. The support received through these partnerships helps us better secure our assets and the information exchange is mutually beneficial to all partners.

Measuring Effectiveness and Performance Assurance

In order to maintain a prepared, unified, and accountable security operation, the Port Authority regularly measures, audits and inspects programs and systems. This practice instills a culture of evaluating the effectiveness and integrity of our systems and program performance. The OCSO also maintains its own Quality Assurance Inspections program that evaluates the physical protection strategies employed at the Port Authority. These internal auditing programs allow us to proactively identify and mitigate issues and concerns before our adversaries exploit them.

Furthermore, in an effort to ensure independent third party review of our security programs, the Port Authority actively participates in the U.S. Department of Homeland Security (DHS) Safety Act program. To date, Port Authority received six (6) awards for designation and one (1) for certification at various facilities.

For 2015, TSA has awarded the PATH Security program its Gold Standard for best practices in rail security.

III. How the Federal Government Can help?

Grant Funding

The Port Authority keeps security as a top priority as evidenced by the investments in resources it makes to that purpose. Currently, agency-wide, 24 percent of personnel and 22 percent of the operating budget is allocated to security. Since 2002, $1.3 billion has been spent in capital security projects and another $900 million in capital security projects have been identified for the coming years.

The Port Authority does not receive any tax dollar support from New York or New Jersey and relies on agency generated revenues to support our operations and capital program. So much of those resources are claimed by maintaining our assets in a state of good repair. Therefore, making Federal grant funding programs even more important to our efforts to secure aging critical infrastructure from evolving threats.

A large source of funds for our capital security projects comes from the Transit Security Grant Program (TSGP). In 2016, the maximum amount of Federal funding through this program was set at $87 million nationwide for all transit operators. This amount, when distributed, can only fund smaller capital security projects. An increase in TSGP funding would allow transit operators to pursue larger capital security projects that would better reduce the risk to those who use our facilities.

We are appreciative of the efforts underway to extend grant durations to allow for delivery of complex security enhancements.

IV. Closing Remarks

In closing, I would like to thank the members of the Surface Transportation and Merchant Marine Infrastructure, Safety and Security subcommittee for inviting me to testify on behalf of the Port Authority of New York and New Jersey.

The Port Authority operates the busiest and most important transportation facilities in the region, as such, we take on the tremendous responsibility of maintaining safety and security. The Port Authority will continue to make enhancements to its policing and security programs and systems in an effort to stay current and adapt to the ever-changing threat landscape. I would like to thank our congressional delegation for their continuing support that allows us to better serve our employees and customers and better protect our regional critical transportation infrastructure.

Senator FISCHER. Thank you, sir, and my thanks to you and all your officers for the work you do daily to protect thousands and thousands of Americans and keep us safe. Thank you.

Mr. BELFIORE. Thank you, ma'am.

Senator FISCHER. To begin with the first round of questions, I'd like to explore cybersecurity. We heard two gentlemen bring up cybersecurity in their comments, and I think that's something that this committee is interested in, and a number of other committees here in the Senate are as well. I serve on the Armed Services Committee, and cybersecurity is a big topic that we are looking at as well.

So, Mr. Straquadine, in your testimony, you mentioned the growing concern with cybersecurity. Could you elaborate a little bit upon that and how not only you work with the Federal Government but if that partnership is open and beneficial, but also how you work with other private entities and if you are able to share information back and forth in order to better combat the threats that are out there?

Mr. STRAQUADINE. Thank you, Chairwoman. Certainly, we work with the agencies—TSA with the responsibility for oversight—but we were approached specifically by Federal Energy Regulatory Commission Chairman Bay. He had stood up a team of Office of Energy Infrastructure Security that had the expertise. They do have regulatory oversight for the electric utilities. They had done these reviews within the utility world.

We were one of the first pipelines to welcome them in, with TSA, to do this review, because we knew we could learn from that. There are many things you know and many things you don't know. The cyber world is ever-changing. So it was one that—coming in with that review—that was well defined up front as a collaborative, non-regulatory approach.

It was one that we shared—or we brought down our information systems experts. Our CEO sat at the table for two days to review this information, because, ultimately, he needs to make the budget decisions to our board. And from that side of things, it was very positive. In fact, I had my information security team come to me and say, "That was the best thing we've ever done," because we could identify the immediate and near-term threats and develop a plan and budget related to that.

We also monitor the information security side that the TSA has as far as their computer centers, or ICS–CERT centers, that are available from a point of view of what's threatening industry, in general, and we do share within our industry within the INGAA association. We've done a——

Senator FISCHER. When you receive a threat, when you antici-
pate a threat, when you hear chatter that's out there of possibili-
ties of a threat to your infrastructure, you're able to share that
with other companies?

Mr. STRAQUADINE. Yes, we are.

Senator FISCHER. And do you also share that with the Federal
Government?

Mr. STRAQUADINE. I believe we do through the ICS–CERT process. We have not had that specific threat. We've recognized no in-
cremental or unique threats to our industry sector to date. But
we're aware, and we will utilize that process as necessary.

Senator FISCHER. And in your testimony, you said that the TSA
clearly acknowledged that they had much to learn in the
cybersecurity realm. What advice would you give to the TSA, and
what advice would you give to this committee about what the priorities should be with regard to cybersecurity?

Mr. STRAQUADINE. I believe the approach of collaboration with
companies to review their cyber approach with experts in the field—
and, clearly, that's where the FERC team has demonstrated that
expertise and has been supportive of doing this effort, again,
collaboratively reaching across to the agency at TSA. It's unique,
as I understand it, in the government, but it's one that has worked
well, at least from what we've perceived and experienced, and what
we've encouraged our industry to participate in as well.

Senator FISCHER. Thank you.

Mr. Spear, you in your comments just briefly stated that you
would like to discuss cybersecurity and would take any questions.
So I'm giving you that opportunity.

Mr. SPEAR. Certainly. I'd look at the trucking industry as quite
vast. It's becoming much more integrated as we adopt electronic
logging devices. The ability to manage fleets nationwide, track
them, manage them in a safe and productive manner requires technology, and that technology is also in the backbone of a network
that could be vulnerable.

We've had instances of ransom ware, servers held for ransom,
stolen customer data. We've had instances where we've done tests
on the ability to access a commercial vehicle's brakes and accelera-
tors. I know this committee has focused a lot of time——

Senator FISCHER. You said you did a test on that. That has been—
—

Mr. SPEAR. There have been researchers at the University of
Michigan that have done a test to determine the ability to hack
into an industrial vehicle's accelerator and braking system. So our
industry is very focused on this issue, like the auto OEMs. I know
there has been a lot of attention on this committee given to the
autos, seeing that there have been instances where vehicles have
been hacked and control has been taken externally from the driver.
Imagine that happening to an 80,000-pound commercial vehicle.
That's something we certainly want to avoid.

We're obviously watching very closely the autonomous debate.
It's an issue that we are coming to the table on. As an industry
working with our OEMs, our software providers, our equipment
providers, we see great promise to safety and environment—less

fuel burned, less congestion, driver retention. There are a lot of benefits that could come out of this technology.

But I think cybersecurity certainly is a question that we believe needs to be answered up front. We're watching very closely what the FCC does in terms of rewarding seven channels of safety spectrum. We would like to see all seven channels go to safety, not shared spectrum with Wi-Fi users. We don't feel that that's something that we want to have compromised in the operation of any vehicle, including commercial vehicles. So this is a space where we believe we need to do more as an industry and be certain that any integration of our systems are not made vulnerable to outside interests and taken advantage of, either for data or the control, actually, of a commercial vehicle.

Senator FISCHER. Thank you very much.

Senator Booker?

Senator BOOKER. With your permission, Chairman Fischer, Senator Blumenthal has some conflicting commitments, and I would like him to go before me.

Senator FISCHER. Of course.

STATEMENT OF HON. RICHARD BLUMENTHAL, U.S. SENATOR FROM CONNECTICUT

Senator BLUMENTHAL. Thank you very, very much, Senator Booker. I appreciate that courtesy, and thank you to both you and the Subcommittee Chairwoman, Senator Fischer, for having this hearing.

Before I begin, I really want to commend both of you for your leadership and your efforts as Chairman and Ranking Member of this committee in your work on the Surface Transportation and Maritime Security Act—very, very important advance. Sorry that it won't be passed during this session, but I think it gives us a template for the next session, and I'm hoping that we can bring it across the finish line next year.

I also want to join in your remarks, Senator Booker, in effect, really lamenting the potential rollback that we see in the CR on trucking safety and fatigue rules, which is very, very unfortunate. I hope that we can remedy that point in the next session as well. And, finally, to echo your concern, Madam Chairwoman, on the issue of cyber, as a member of the Armed Services Committee, you'll recall that in our hearing recently with a number of very expert witnesses on emerging threats and national security, cyber was at the forefront, and both Senator McCain and I attended a briefing of the Senate United States Marine Corps Caucus, where the commandant's major concern, his priority, was, in fact, or is now cyber and the prospect of cyber attack and the need for cyber defense. So all of our systems, utilities, finance, medical, and transportation very much implicate the issue of cybersecurity.

I want to ask a question that involves the TSA, specifically, the implementing recommendation of the 9/11 Commission Act, which dates from 2007. That law required the Department of Homeland Security, through the TSA, to take rigorous, robust action to stem the tide of terrorist threats to transportation on our shores, including the surface transportation network.

A lot of the focus has been on our skies and aviation security, but the law required TSA to complete a number of critical security mandates by August 2008 regarding rail and surface transportation. And to be very blunt, the TSA is nowhere near completing the necessary actions that will help protect rail stations, transit facilities, bus stops, and other critical points of transit and to prevent attacks on soft targets throughout our surface transportation network.

There are three specific areas of concern that I have: number one, ensuring high-risk target railroads have sufficient security plans; number two, training, ensuring that public transportation agencies, railroads, and bus providers have training standards on security threats for their frontline employees; and, number three, vetting, ensuring that public transportation agencies and railroads conduct rigorous name-based security background checks and immigration status checks on all frontline employees.

TSA, unfortunately, has met none of these statutory requirements. They are legal requirements in our statutes. And I'm very concerned about this fact and have repeatedly demanded answers from TSA about when it's going to comply with the law, and the repeated answer has been, "It's hard. It takes time." But in the meantime, what we see around the country and around the world is, in fact, attacks on the soft targets, whether they are the perimeters outside checkpoints at airports or some of our rail and rail facilities and threats to them.

Mr. Roth, you share my many concerns, and in your testimony, you referred to the DHS as—I'm quoting—"dismissive and lax," end quote, in implementing requirements. Is this particularly troubling after these attacks that we've seen at train stations and rail stations around the world, and how do we get DHS to take action?

Mr. ROTH. I share your concern with this, and certainly in my testimony—we put a chart in the back of my testimony that shows the delays that TSA has had, notwithstanding the fact that there have been numerous high profile rail attacks, starting, in fact, with the 2004 Madrid attacks, that were very concerning. The regulations that are required under the 9/11 Commission Act are all very common sense, and it would really bring rail transportation on par with air transportation.

An airport has to have a security plan that's approved by DHS. It seems common sense for railroads to have the same. Airport workers have to have a background check that includes terrorism screening. It seems very common sense that railroad workers would have to have this. We pressed TSA on exactly what the delay is, and we didn't get a good answer. We've got, I think, the same answer that you have received, which is that rulemaking is difficult. Yet they've made rules with regard to airports, and they've made rules with regard to seaports, but they somehow have not yet gone to surface. So I do share your frustration.

Senator BLUMENTHAL. And as you're aware—and Mr. Trugman is especially aware—Penn Station actually handles half a million passengers every day. Senator Booker and I are often among them, or at least he is a rider of Amtrak. I know I see him there all the time. But I go in and out of Penn Station, and I sometimes wonder when I do, whether the security is adequate. I see some of it there.

There's no question that some of that security is visible in the form of police and K–9s. It's the busiest transportation hub in our country, busier than all three airports combined.

My question to you, Mr. Trugman, is: Is Penn Station—Amtrak owns it—really prepared?

Mr. TRUGMAN. We are prepared, and we work really well with our partners. It's a layered approach. All our employees are trained. All our passengers—you see the videos that we have when you're boarding the train. I thank you for your ridership. Those are all part of the training that we get through the DHS grant in our emergency corporate communications—corporate security administration which we have, the EMCS.

You know, we work very closely with our NYPD, with the New York State Police, and all the law enforcement community. The intelligence that we get—because we're embedded in the JTTF in New York and the national JTTF—is vital to protecting that. The K–9 program is a very important part of that strategy, and our counter measures with the counter-terrorism units that we have is very—it's a layered approach, and we work well with that.

Senator BLUMENTHAL. And you would not disagree with Mr. Roth that those TSA regulations are important?

Mr. TRUGMAN. They're very important. But right now, we have a great working relationship with TSA. We have the VIPR teams that come to the stations, the FAMS that work in the stations, not only in New York but across Amtrak. We work really well with the Office of Intelligence for TSA. We're doing pilot projects with the TSA Office of Requirement Capabilities Assessment. We have an MOU with them. So we have a good working relationship with the TSA.

Senator BLUMENTHAL. I have a great working relationship with the TSA, too. I admire the dedicated individuals who work there, and I try to tell them all the time whenever I see them, in the airports, particularly, how much I appreciate their hard work. They are under-resourced, regulations are hard to do, and they do take time. I just want them to do that part of their job a little bit more expeditiously. But I share your respect for them.

Thank you, Madam Chairwoman.

Senator FISCHER. Thank you, Senator Blumenthal.

Senator Klobuchar?

STATEMENT OF HON. AMY KLOBUCHAR, U.S. SENATOR FROM MINNESOTA

Senator KLOBUCHAR. Thank you very much, Madam Chairman, and thank you, Ranking Member Booker, for this hearing.

The terror threat against the commuter rail station in L.A. yesterday reminds us that our transportation systems are still a target. In fact, in an article in 2014 in al-Qaeda and the Arabian Peninsula's terror recruitment magazine, *Inspire,* the magazine provided instructions on how to make a bomb using non-metallic materials, how to bypass TSA security, and all of you know all too well, the threat that we face here. So that's why I appreciate this hearing.

I want to take us a little away from where maybe most of the people have been focused on, and this is to the Canadian border, which borders my state. The Canadian National Railway border crossing just east of International Falls in Minnesota sees the most railroad cars of any crossing between the U.S. and Canada, and you know $2 billion of goods go back and forth between the two countries every single day and 350,000 passengers.

The improving economy and increased demand for imports and Canadian crude oil has created a rail bottleneck at our Minnesota-Ontario rail crossing. I've heard from my constituents about significant delays. Some of the trains are nearly two miles long and represent a challenge for people getting to work and emergency vehicles that need to pass.

I guess I'd start with you, Inspector General. How is TSA working with other government agencies and local partners to address safety and efficiency, and what are some of the biggest challenges that TSA faces?

Mr. ROTH. Certainly, when it comes to ports of entry, particularly land ports of entry on the northern border, Customs and Border Protection has the lion's share of the role in ensuring the efficient transport of people and material across the border while at the same time maintaining security, and it is an enormous challenge. Having toured the northern border, including the Port of Detroit, which is also a very, very busy port——

Senator KLOBUCHAR. I've been there, yes.

Mr. ROTH. They have enormous challenges, both with manpower, with infrastructure, and the kinds of increases that are necessary as trade increases. So I'm deeply sympathetic to the CBP mission there and the challenges that they face. They seem to manage, but I understand that there are challenges.

Senator KLOBUCHAR. Right. Exactly.

My next question is, I guess, for you, Mr. Belfiore, as well as the Inspector General. So what we passed last week, the Cross Border Trade Facilitation Act, was a bill that Senator Cornyn and I have led, which allows for public-private partnerships to help improve infrastructure and increase the number of Customs and Border Patrol inspectors at our land ports of entry. There is significant support in the House as well, and we believe this is going to become law. There have been trials, and now this would permanently allow for these partnerships.

CBP has a $5 billion budget shortfall, and that's why we think engaging private partners to fill the gap for places where they see this need for extra commerce security is helpful. As I mentioned, we've got some major ports of entry in our state.

Given budget constraints, I guess I would start with you, Mr. Belfiore. How do you think this legislation can best be used to improve transportation security at our ports of entry—points of entry and ports?

Mr. BELFIORE. So in speaking to those that run the ports for the Port Authority of New York and New Jersey and particularly those who are interested in security—of course, we have a strong partnership with CBP and the U.S. Coast Guard in what we do in trying to secure the ports. We think that additional CBP presence is very important for the success of that security program that we have.

In addition to that, there's also a business impact to the presence of CBP in addition to, first and foremost, security. It would allow for greater throughput and allow for probably more hours of operation that would accommodate the growth that the ports of New Jersey are currently experiencing.

Senator KLOBUCHAR. Very good. Just turning to my last question here on rail safety—and, by the way, I want to welcome Mr. Straquadine—thank you so much—with the Natural Gas Association of America, and Minnesota has a company. Thank you very much. We appreciate that.

Mr. STRAQUADINE. Thank you, Senator.

Senator KLOBUCHAR. We move more than a million barrels of oil by rail every day in Minnesota, and transporting hazardous materials can pose a significant risk to surrounding communities. And, of course, I hear concerns all the time from communities, Inspector General, about delays, but also about risks, and, of course, we've had some spills of not just oil, but biofuels and other things over the years in Minnesota, Wisconsin. I think people don't realize because of where we are how much traffic we get from North Dakota and Canada and other places.

We pushed in the FAST Act to have provisions to help local governments to plan and respond to rail incidents. But I just wondered if you could give an update on what training or collaboration TSA is using with state and local security partners for derailments or hazardous spills.

Mr. ROTH. The authority for this is actually split between TSA as well as the Federal Emergency Management Administration, FEMA. FEMA focuses much on what would occur in a response sort of environment, and we have not looked at that specific issue. I know that the General Accountability Office is currently looking at how FEMA is doing through that kind of collaboration to determine whether or not they are prepared in the event of oil spills.

I will have to say on the other part of it, the TSA part of it, the surface transportation part of what TSA does has been largely ignored by TSA. The focus has been almost exclusively on aviation security and, candidly, almost exclusively on checkpoint security, not even sort of insider threat kinds of security as well. So the kinds of things that they could do, they've missed the opportunities to do, including sharing intelligence, sharing best practices, the kinds of things that would prevent a spill from occurring in the first place.

Senator KLOBUCHAR. Right. So you're talking about best practices and more people at these locations, the facilities, which is what Senator Cornyn and I are trying to get at with our bill, when it comes to rail, is what you want to see.

Mr. ROTH. That's correct.

Senator KLOBUCHAR. Very good.

Do you want to add anything—our local guy?

Mr. STRAQUADINE. I would just add that the challenge around transportation of energy by rail is overcome by long-term commitments to pipeline installations. While I represent the natural gas industry, specifically Alliance Pipeline, the fact is that oil by pipe is the safest, most efficient, and cost effective way to move energy from a producing region to a consuming or refining area.

Senator KLOBUCHAR. And we have, as you know, some major refineries in our state.

Mr. STRAQUADINE. Yes, we do.

Senator KLOBUCHAR. So some upgrades to the pipelines.

Mr. STRAQUADINE. We do have wonderful oversight by the Department of Transportation Pipelines Hazardous Material Safety Administration that we work collaboratively with, from our company's perspective, but much like we did in our cybersecurity review with TSA and FERC. We reach out to PHMSA to find best ways to learn how we can do things better and how we can encourage them to look at best practices as well.

Senator KLOBUCHAR. Thank you very much.

Thank you, everyone.

Thank you, Chief, as well.

Senator FISCHER. Thank you, Senator Klobuchar.

Senator Booker?

Senator BOOKER. Just really quickly, a small issue but very irksome, Mr. Belfiore. The Port Authority of New York and New Jersey—shouldn't it be called the Port Authority of New Jersey and New York?

[Laughter.]

Mr. BELFIORE. I'll take that back, Senator.

Senator KLOBUCHAR. This is like Fargo-Moorhead should be called Moorhead-Fargo.

Senator BOOKER. I just want to make sure to get that on the record, sir.

Mr. BELFIORE. Yes, sir.

Senator FISCHER. We need to make a lot of changes.

Senator KLOBUCHAR. Yes, we need to make some changes right here.

Senator BOOKER. Yes, right now, on the record. Let the record reflect that he said he will go back and change that immediately.

[Laughter.]

Senator BOOKER. Look, I have, like the good Senator from Connecticut, a lot of respect for TSA and their workers. I interact with them on a regular basis as my course of travel. But, obviously, I'm very frustrated with some of the larger issues in regards to the TSA. The agency has stated for years that they use an intelligence-driven, risk-based strategy for transportation security. But a recent DHS Inspector General report found that the agency does not have a risk-based strategy across transportation modes. This is very concerning to me.

So, in your opinion, Mr. Belfiore, what are the consequences for security for surface transportation, of the TSA not using a risk-based strategy?

Mr. BELFIORE. So, in being familiar with the IG's report and Mr. Roth's report, I think it includes many important recommendations. But, perhaps to me, the most important recommendation is the adoption of an intelligence-led, risk-based strategy across all of the areas of responsibility for TSA.

I think that it's something that our office and the Port Authority can wrestle with every day, as we are multimodal, and there are only so many dollars, and we compete with the importance of maintaining those critical assets and keeping them in a state of good repair and taking those same dollars and creating new development of very important transportation assets, and at the same time, we need to secure what we have. The best way to spend those precious dollars, we think, is with the intelligence-led, risk-based methodology that we have.

So what it does for us is it looks for risks and threat and vulnerability. It looks at what's in place to defend those assets.

Senator BOOKER. I'm sorry to cut you off. This is what frustrates me—and you are so gracious in being grateful to the Congress for the grants that you all get for security. But my opinion is that we are trying to do a lot with very little, because we're not allocating our resources based upon the threats to our country.

More people travel the Northeast corridor by rail than they do by air. In addition to that, if you look at the targets in the greater New York area, which is the number one target, arguably, for terrorists—at least it's ranked that way by the Department of Homeland Security as a high-risk region—you understand—if you look at it in analysis of all the attacks being carried out globally right now, since 2001, more than 1,900 attacks have been carried out against public transportation systems globally, resulting in 4,000 deaths, 14,000 injuries. The attacks on metro stations, on rails—this year, the attack on the Brussels metro station killed more than a dozen people and injured more.

If we look at the pattern of attacks, globally, right now, you're seeing them disproportionately focused on the transportation modes that you're charged with protecting. Yet the resources and the allocation of those resources are being put in a way that seems to be contrary to any evidence-based analysis of where we need to shore up these soft targets.

So the persistent threat to rail, to public transportation, is not reflected in grant funding. In your opinion—and I know how grateful you are for the Federal grant funding you get—does the current amount of grant funding reflect the need that your agency has for protecting vulnerable targets?

Mr. BELFIORE. Well, the short answer to that, Senator, is no.

Senator BOOKER. OK. And I'm mindful of my time, but, to me, that really does turn us to your written testimony, which is, to me, just shocking. It's actually shocking, your testimony, to be able to say that we have a real problem, that we have resources being poured into protecting from the last terrorist attack, focusing on what has happened and not looking at the pattern of what the enemy is actually doing. To me, that is highly frustrating and alarming, that even when the 9/11 Commission clearly states the problem, we have done nothing almost a decade later. Missing deadline after deadline, we've done nothing to effectuate it.

Being that I savor my bipartisan relationship with Chairman Fischer, my time has expired. I'm going to stop and keep going. The graciousness of—let the record show that——

Senator FISCHER. He's on a roll.

Senator BOOKER. So Congress actually passed legislation. I feel like we're being responsible. And you said this, again, in your testimony. We passed legislation about implementing the 9/11 recommendations. So there were several requirements in law for TSA to issue regulations. This is astounding to me, that by law, they've been required to issue regulations that would provide direction to public transportation agencies, railroads, bus companies on security training for frontline transportation workers.

Your review, Mr. Roth, is so alarming, and I just want to understand. I mean, I know what would happen, God forbid, if what we see happening in European nation after European nation were to happen here in the United States. But that's not what I want. I don't want to be able to have people say, "I told you so." We need to get the job done and protect surface transportation. Eight years after a law was passed, 8 years, and the TSA has yet to issue proposed rules to implement the 9/11 Commission's recommendations. So my first question to you is: What are the consequences, in your opinion, or potential consequences, of their lack of action? And your job as an IG is—is the TSA in any way back on track to implementing those regulations?

Mr. ROTH. To answer your last question first, they are not. They can't give us a date as to when even they will submit the regulations to OMB, which is, as you know, the first step in a process of a long rulemaking process. So it's not even out of the building yet for two of the most important of those regulations. So I share your frustration with that. And, really, what it is—it's illustrative of TSA, when they talk about being risk-based, what they're talking about is they risk base the passengers who come through screening. But they don't do any risk-based approach to anything else that they do as part of their job.

To give an example, they have the Federal Air Marshal Service, which is a program that—the actual budget is classified, but it's in the hundreds of millions of dollars, multiple hundreds of millions of dollars for this program, for Federal Air Marshals to sit there to ensure that nobody enters a cockpit whose doors are locked. So the question is what risk, exactly, are they trying to counter here? And the cost of that program is astronomical.

So why aren't they, as sort of an entity, taking a look at what are your threats, what is it we can do to counter those threats, and then let's build a budget that will actually make sense to counter those threats with programs that they put in place. They have not done that. So it is particularly sort of disingenuous for them to call themselves an intelligence-driven, risk-based organization when, in fact, they are not, not only across modes of transportation, but even within air transportation.

Senator BOOKER. So, I mean, this is—I don't understand why this sense of alarm is not greater in our country when, again, we're watching the attacks our enemy is doing in other nations. It's astonishing to me that we would—even the monies we are allocating are so misallocated in proportion to what the actual threats are.

This is not being done in an intelligent manner. This is not being done in a systematic manner. It's not following Federal regulations. It's not following Federal law. I mean, I'm not sure if I'm seeing what seems to appear to me to be willful disregard for the security and the safety of our Nation by an agency so out of line, eight years out of line, with the Congressional mandates.

You've been in this business for a long time. Give me some recommendation about what Congress could be doing to get this agency on track to protect the American people.

Mr. ROTH. I wish I had some sort of silver bullet for you. I think it's continued oversight, as I said in my testimony, by the Congress, by my office, by the Government Accountability Office. I don't have any good answers for you.

Senator BOOKER. You know, the people to your left, sir, from the private industry to the sworn officers—they go out there every single day, trying to protect Americans. You know, I don't always agree with industry, as you heard from the beginning. But, dear God, they're trying to keep their product safe and people safe. And I see this from what happened in Elizabeth, from what happened in Manhattan, that the threat isn't gone. People are plotting right now, right now, against this country, and we can't even make an intelligent allocation of the assets we have and, arguably, from the documents that you produced, are wasting millions of dollars, as you said, with the security at doors, for a problem that could be solved on a fraction of the cost and that money reinvested into principal targets.

So I don't need another round. The last question I have, to shift a little bit—Chief, I worry about—obviously, I'm a New Jersey Senator, and I've seen what happened on 9/11, literally watching it with my own eyes from where I stood in Newark, and I worry about critical infrastructure not having redundancy.

So it has been billed as an infrastructure project, the rail lines across the Hudson, the ones that are now crumbling, in one of the most critical economic arteries of our country—20 percent of our GDP in this region. Just for—quickly, because I'm definitely treading on the grace of my colleague—can you just—and this will be my final question. Why are those tunnels not just important for infrastructure and the flow of commerce and goods, but why are they important for the security of the region?

Mr. TRUGMAN. Well, they're very important. And, as you, I was a young kid growing up in Brooklyn, New York, and watched the building of those two towers. I never thought I'd watch them crumble as a D.C. police officer. So I changed my whole aspect in law enforcement that day.

The Gateway project and the tunnels they have now—we do—again, I'll reference my layered approach. We have a layered approach where we do right-of-way patrol to protect those tunnels and the infrastructure that goes into Manhattan from New Jersey. We have worked with our partners in Amtrak, with the Emergency Management And Corporate Security office for video systems, intrusion systems. We work very closely with our partners. I can't stress that enough, from everything—I have a detective assigned to the New Jersey Fusion Center. I have detectives assigned to the JTTFs, as I testified. We work with our partners at the New Jersey-New York Port Authority Police Department, the New Jersey Transit Police, the New Jersey State Police—just about every jurisdiction you can imagine.

Together, that's what keeps us safe, because we all work together. We host meetings—the Northeast Corridor Coalition with the intelligence groups from every jurisdiction, basically, now, from Washington to Boston, to discuss what we're seeing and what we need to prepare for. So I am confident what we're doing is everything we possibly can do right now, because the infrastructure, not just the tunnels, but the bridges, are very concerning.

We work with the marine units from the New Jersey State Police, from the D.C. Police Department to check some of the bridges here in the city, and the aviation units. We've talked to our aviation partners in the military and the police departments to look out for our tracks. It's a simple—I get a call from an aviation pilot who says, "What do I look for?" I say, "Anybody who's not wearing a hard hat or an orange jacket or an orange shirt doesn't belong there." So it's that simple, and that's what we do.

Senator BOOKER. Thank you, sir.

Thank you, Madam Chairwoman.

Senator FISCHER. Thank you, Senator Booker. I'm going to do a little cleanup if that's OK with you.

Mr. Roth, to follow up with my colleague's line of questioning and his expressed frustration, do you think that the TSA is even structured correctly? Do you have any comments on that?

Mr. ROTH. We haven't looked at that as a specific issue. I know that, historically, before the current administrator of TSA was there, it was a fairly stove-piped organization. Certainly, when we looked at ground transportation security, it seemed that that was stove-piped. In other words, there's a Chief Risk Officer who is supposed to be looking at risk enterprise-wide. We were able to show him documents, TSA documents, that he had never seen before with regard to ground transportation risk.

So there are certain stove pipes certainly within TSA. We don't have any recommendations as to how to fix that, at least in these reports.

Senator FISCHER. Thank you.

Mr. Spear, some questions for you. In your written testimony—and to follow up what Mr. Roth was talking about right now with security at airports—you mentioned that the DOD allows workers to transit in and out of military facilities with their TWIC in lieu of additional credentials. Do you think that's secure, first of all? And, second, how does it affect efficiency?

Mr. SPEAR. Well, I do think it's secure. I actually had a common access card with the DOD for a number of years. I've used it all over the world, used it in the green zone in Iraq. It's a phenomenal ID. It's great protocol, great command control over the system. It's an outstanding example of how to get it right.

Now, why we can't do the same thing with TWIC is beyond me. I can tell you that after we left Iraq, the Iraqi government adopted the same ID system that common access card utilizes. This is my ID for the green zone, Iraqi ID, same chip, same biometrics, same credentialing, and same protocol. Now, I would argue that the Iraqi government is not a bastion for efficiency, but why they are doing it better than TWIC is beyond me.

So I think it's a living example of why—you know, to have to wait 15 years since MTSA was enacted, 9 years since the TWIC rule became final and effective, and we still have to wait two more years for the reader rule to become final—I mean, how long does it take to do an ID card?

Senator FISCHER. You have a lot of different credentials that drivers have to go through. I've got a list here. You've got the

TWIC. You've got the HME, which is hazardous material endorsement. You have the free and secure trade.

Mr. SPEAR. That's correct.

Senator FISCHER. Do drivers need all those? What is it like for a driver to have to go through that process in time and energy and cost? And let's get back to what we're worried about here with security. Does it take all of these cards to make a driver more secure?

Mr. SPEAR. In our opinion, no. As I said earlier, I think pro‑tecting the homeland, to have a system that's seamless yet se‑ cure—we've proven it. The common access card proves it. We have living examples. We have other agencies like DOD that allow TWIC to be used on base. Now, if we're allowing drivers to access military installations with a TWIC card, I can't understand why TSA can't get past this impediment and use it seamlessly across the board for all MTSA facilities. It just doesn't make any sense to me.

Our drivers, for instance, are frustrated by it. Right now, they do need all these IDs. We would argue that they should have one, and that it should be seamless, and it's proven that it can be done securely. Our drivers—you know, to go through the process to ob‑tain an HME or a TWIC card—it takes time, and if you put your‑self in the role of a driver, they're out driving. That's their job. So to take time to go to an enrollment center and to go through this process is taking them out of a situation where they're earning money and going through this process to obtain the credential.

It has gotten more efficient, I will say. Since we last testified be‑fore the Senate in 2014, the cost has come down, the enrollment centers are much more widespread, and the time that it takes, from 6 to 8 weeks, has actually been reported in the field as a little more than two weeks in many instances. So there are some pockets of improvement, but it's not across the board.

I would also say that when they go to the enrollment centers, there's a lack of parking. For a truck driver, that's also a problem. So we have a truck driving parking problem nationwide already, especially in the Northeast Corridor. These enrollment centers don't accommodate that, either. So there are a lot of impediments that they have to go through to get that.

But I think the real underlining thing that I would say is that we have a chronic driver shortage. So for carriers that are trying to get drivers to move hazardous cargo and go to these particular sites that require multiple credentialing, it's very problematic, very disruptive to their business, very disruptive to the customers and to commerce, in general. So these are impediments that I believe could easily be solved if we'd just adopt TWIC universally.

Senator FISCHER. Thank you, Mr. Spear.

Senator Booker, did you have other questions?

Senator BOOKER. Besides reminding Chief Trugman that when he talks about New York-New Jersey transportation, it's not the tunnels that go into Manhattan. It's actually the tunnels that go into New Jersey, sir. So you should prioritize that understanding.

[Laughter.]

Mr. TRUGMAN. I stand corrected.

Senator BOOKER. Thank you very much, sir.

Senator FISCHER. I see a common thread here today going through.

Senator BOOKER. It's true. These New Yorkers don't understand. But even their football teams don't play, actually, in New York. They play in New Jersey, which is God's country, sir.

[Laughter.]

Mr. TRUGMAN. There's only one team that actually plays in New York right now, and that's the Buffalo Bills.

Senator BOOKER. Yes, yes. I'm glad you understand that. Thank you, sir.

Senator FISCHER. Thank you, Senator Booker.

I would like to note that the hearing record will remain open for two weeks, and during that time Senators are asked to submit any questions for the record. Upon receipt, the witnesses are requested to submit their written answers to the Committee as soon as possible.

With that, I would like to thank all of you for being here today. I appreciate you taking the time to offer us some valuable information.

The hearing is adjourned.

[Whereupon, at 4:10 p.m., the hearing was adjourned.]

APPENDIX

RESPONSE TO WRITTEN QUESTION SUBMITTED BY HON. JOHN THUNE TO
HON. JOHN ROTH

Question. How is TSA progressing towards a risk-based strategy for non-aviation transportation systems. Your September 9 report identified TSA's deficiencies in this area and made several recommendations. I concurred with your concerns and in September introduced the Surface Transportation and Maritime Security Act which would require TSA to develop a risk-based strategy. Have you seen progress from TSA in developing a strategy that first identifies the risks and then determines the proper funding levels?

Answer. On November 21, 2016, TSA provided us with an update on the actions it has taken to address the recommendations in our report, *TSA Needs a Cross-cutting Risk-Based Security Strategy* (OIG–16–134). TSA indicated that it expects to complete a risk-based security strategy that encompasses all transportation modes in the fourth quarter of FY 2017. TSA is also taking steps to integrate enterprise risk management with resource planning and expects to complete this process by December 31, 2020. We will continue to monitor TSA's progress on addressing our recommendations.

RESPONSE TO WRITTEN QUESTIONS SUBMITTED BY HON. DEB FISCHER TO
HON. JOHN ROTH

Question 1. Mr. Roth, you referenced the 9/11 Act and that TSA has not fulfilled several rail security directives, including identifying high risk carriers. Has the TSA indicated its intention to carry out these directives and strengthen rail security?

Answer. On November 29, 2016, TSA provided us with an update to the recommendations we made in our report, *TSA Oversight of National Passenger Rail System Security* (OIG–16–91). TSA has designated the rulemakings as high priority and indicated it is making progress. On December 16, 2016, TSA published two rulemakings in the *Federal Register:*

- *Notice of Proposed Rulemaking for Security Training for Surface Transportation Employees* and
- *Advance Notice of Proposed Rulemaking for Surface Transportation Vulnerability Assessments and Security Plans.*

TSA anticipates a Notice of Proposed Rulemaking for surface security vetting by the end of 2017.

Question 2. There are concerns about the GAO's recommendations for "alternative" credentialing methods, including the potential for a decentralized system (whereby each entity have their own port security systems). Can you elaborate further on these concerns?

Answer. We did not review "alternative" credentialing methods in our audit, *TWIC Background Checks are Not as Reliable as They Could Be* (OIG–16–128). However, during site visits at two ports, we observed that port workers were required to have a valid TWIC as well as airport issued credential to access certain port areas. We believe there could be increased security risks if TSA adopts "alternative" credentialing methods because the Department would have to provide oversight to ensure the decentralized credentialing methods meet minimum security requirements.

Question 3. What are your thoughts on the United States Coast Guard's (USCG) August 2016 final rule that will require high-risk category facilities and a vessel to incorporate an electronic TWIC validation process, which includes a biometric check for high-risk category facilities and a vessel, prior to entry into a secured area?

Answer. The final rule was published after we completed our audit field work. Additionally, TWIC implementation at facilities and vessels was outside the scope of our review, which focused on the TSA background check process. GAO identified in its 2011 audit that unless TSA strengthens its background check process, there is a risk that someone can access a secured area with a fraudulently obtained TWIC card whether or not the facility uses a card reader. We agree with GAO's assessment.

Question 4. The August 2016 TWIC reader rule also states that, while not required, a maritime operator can utilize electronic TWIC inspection on a voluntary basis if they feel that this provides an additional level of security protection—and many have chosen to incorporate TWIC electronic readers into their USCG facility security plans. Are you seeing the biometric check being utilized beyond the category facilities that will be subject to USCG Final Rule?

Answer. Voluntary use of electronic card readers was outside the scope of our audit. We attempted to obtain a listing of all facilities that use electronic card readers for background informational purposes only; however, USCG officials told us they were unable to provide that information. We may pursue this topic during a future audit.

———

RESPONSE TO WRITTEN QUESTION SUBMITTED BY HON. CORY BOOKER TO HON. JOHN ROTH

Question. The Federal Government has a vital role in ensuring that freight flow is not inhibited by a lack of security resources.

In order for our ports to perform efficiently, U.S. Customs and Border Protection (CBP) must be adequately funded and staffed. In 2015, when CBP was last funded to hire additional staff, only 20 of 2,000 staff were assigned to seaports. In addition to the obvious implications for homeland security, this is also a supply chain problem. When vessels cannot efficiently move through the customs process, the delays can ripple throughout our Nation's supply chain.

Although there is no single solution to port congestion, the gap in Federal investment is an issue that we have the ability to address.

What can Congress do to better match resources with the need to secure our supply chain?

Answer. To determine CBP resources is a complex process. CBP uses a three-pronged resource optimization strategy for improving port operations. The workload staffing model is used to identify CBP's staffing needs at ports of entry. The model takes into account operational data from CBP information technology (IT) systems, as well as information that program offices provide. CBP uses workload staffing model results in its budget requests to increase user fees and request additional staff. In 2014, we issued a report on CBP's workload staffing model, *U.S. Customs and Border Protection's Workload Staffing Model* (OIG–14–117), where we reported that the workload staffing model methodology is sound, but the data from more than 25 IT systems used in calculations may not be reliable. This calls into question predicted staffing needs and shortages. We recommended CBP catalog, track, and validate all data sources; and independently verify and validate version 2 of the workload staffing model after its completion, to ensure that it satisfies CBP's requirements and functions as CBP intended. We are monitoring CBP's implementation of the recommendations and expect completion by January 31, 2017.

To help mitigate staffing and other resource shortages, CBP relies on technology for screening cargo shipments. Specifically, it uses the Automated Targeting System to review, identify, and select cargo shipments that pose a possible threat to national security. Additionally, CBP relies on cross-agency coordination efforts to make the supply chain more efficient. Our report, *CBP's Houston Seaport Generally Complied with Cargo Examination Requirements but Could Improve Its Documentation of Waivers and Exceptions* (OIG–15–64), included recommendations that have strengthened controls in identifying high-risk cargo shipments. CBP has also implemented recommendations in OIG report, *Inspection of U.S. Customs and Border Protection Miami Field Office Ports of Entry* (OIG–15–13) to improve Miami Field Office Port of Entry operations for passenger screening, agriculture safeguarding operations, and cargo targeting.

———

RESPONSE TO WRITTEN QUESTION SUBMITTED BY HON. JOHN THUNE TO NEIL TRUGMAN

Question. Chief Trugman, will you discuss the security challenges of the open environments we see in train stations and what TSA is doing to help you ensure the safety of the traveling public?

Answer. Surface transportation as a whole remains an "open" environment because it provides a functional service for millions of rail passengers and mass transit commuters. Because of the volume and daily use of these systems, the maintenance of accessible and efficient surface transportation is an essential requirement for the travel needs of the public for the present and the future. Multi-modal, major Amtrak stations like New York, Washington D.C., Philadelphia and Chicago alone are utilized by hundreds of thousands of passengers, patrons and members of the public each day. Surface transportation and its "open" environment is, therefore, a key part of this Nation's infrastructure.

Protecting Amtrak's passengers, employees, patrons and infrastructure is challenging. The Amtrak Police Department relies upon a three pronged security philosophy—Prevention, Partnership and Participation. Through these prongs, the Amtrak security platform is established and developed through corporate security plans, Amtrak Police deployments, collaborations with federal, state and local law enforcement stakeholders, training and public outreach programs. The Partnership prong, by necessity, is extremely important to Amtrak because of its Federal mandate to operate an intercity rail system that covers 500 communities in 46 states. With TSA, Amtrak has found one of its most reliable partners to help keep "America's Railroad" safe. Amtrak continues to consider our relationship with TSA as good and supportive of the security strategy that Amtrak employs. The following are examples of the types of regular and ongoing support that TSA provides to Amtrak:

- Provision of TSA National Screening force personnel on a regular basis to major Amtrak stations to supplement Amtrak's random and unpredictable baggage screening program
- Use of FAM personnel to support undercover and surge operations
- Seminal Partner in RAILSAFE program
- APD participates in the TSA Mass Transit Peer Advisory Group (PAG) as part of one of the Sector-Specific Government Coordinating Councils created under the NIPP
- Daily exchange of intelligence and information sharing with TSA–OI and the APD AIT
- Identification of potential security risks and improvements through TSA BASE program
- Participation and support of TSA through HSEEP Exercise programs and training
- Strong programmatic relationship for coordination and support of IPR Grant/CA and NECDT programs
- Relationship with TSA as a Mass Transit Test Bed agency
- Cooperative approach on 49 CFR 1580 compliance regulations

RESPONSE TO WRITTEN QUESTIONS SUBMITTED BY HON. DEB FISCHER TO NEIL TRUGMAN

Question 1. What are your thoughts on the United States Coast Guard's (USCG) August 2016 final rule that will require high-risk category facilities and a vessel to incorporate an electronic TWIC validation process, which includes a biometric check for high-risk category facilities and a vessel, prior to entry into a secured area?

Answer. Amtrak must qualify this response with the fact that it is not typically under USCG regulation and for the most part is not covered by TWIC regulations. As a result, Amtrak's experience is very limited. Since the USCG final rule on mandatory use of electronic TWIC validation process is defined to specific areas—facilities or vessels with certain dangerous cargo (CDC) or with 1,000 or more passengers—it would not seem to apply to Amtrak on most occasions even if such regulations were applicable.

Amtrak would agree generally, however, that use of a biometric check would increase the security levels of a facility or vessel.

Question 2. The August 2016 TWIC reader rule also states that, while not required, a maritime operator can utilize electronic TWIC inspection on a voluntary basis if they feel that this provides an additional level of security protection—and many have chosen to incorporate TWIC electronic readers into their USCG facility security plans. Are you seeing the biometric check being utilized beyond the category facilities that will be subject to USCG Final Rule?

Answer. Again, this does not apply to Amtrak at the current time. Amtrak has not had any experiences in this area to share with the Committee.

RESPONSE TO WRITTEN QUESTION SUBMITTED BY HON. CORY BOOKER TO
NEIL TRUGMAN

Question. The Federal Government has a vital role in ensuring that freight flow is
not inhibited by a lack of security resources. In order for our ports to perform
efficiently, U.S. Customs and Border Protection (CBP) must be adequately funded
and staffed. In 2015, when CBP was last funded to hire additional staff, only 20 of
2,000 staff were assigned to seaports. In addition to the obvious implications for
homeland security, this is also a supply chain problem. When vessels cannot efficiently move through the customs process, the delays can ripple throughout our Nation's supply chain. Although there is no single solution to port congestion, the gap in
Federal investment is an issue that we have the ability to address. What can
Congress do to better match resources with the need to secure our supply chain?
Answer. Seaport and port supply chain security are not areas where the Amtrak
Police Department has typical duties and responsibilities. The Amtrak Intercity
Passenger Rail system does not intersect with vessel and shipping related security
issues as it does with other modes of surface transportation like commuter rail and
busses. However, the Amtrak Police Department does collaborate and address security issues with the USCG, state and local agencies with regard to Amtrak's critical
infrastructure in or over waterways like railroad bridges and buttresses. Solid working relationships are maintained with these law enforcement agencies and security
matters are coordinated.

Generally, Amtrak agrees with the premise that more funding of maritime security programs, like more funding of surface transportation programs, is essential to
improving America's homeland defense and must be a key ingredient to maintaining
and creating programs to prevent all hazards events, including criminal and terrorist acts.

———

RESPONSE TO WRITTEN QUESTION SUBMITTED BY HON. JOHN THUNE TO
CHRIS SPEAR

Question. Mr. Spears, there has been a lot of discussion of the TWIC program.
I hear the program has progressed, but I am interested in your thoughts. Is the
TWIC program providing the verifications you need and how would you like to see
the program changed?
Answer. ATA continues to support the concept of a single, federally-issued credential for transportation workers to satisfy multiple security threat assessment (STA)
requirements. The TWIC is a robust, standardized credential that, when paired with
appropriate card readers, has the potential to serve as a valuable and effective tool
to enhance the security of our ports and other critical infrastructure. Unfortunately,
drivers with TWIC cards are still subjected to multiple, identical STAs to obtain
separate credentials in order to access other highly secure facilities and haul hazardous materials. This has resulted in the costly and inefficient environment that
motor carriers and drivers operate in today. So long as there is no one single, uni-
versally-accepted credential, the full potential of the TWIC cannot be realized.

Under the law, TSA may only perform STAs for a TWIC card on workers "en-
gaged in the field of transportation". Recently, TSA amended its legal interpretation
of "field of transportation" to cover "any individual, activity, entity, facility, owner,
or operator that is subject to regulation by TSA, Department of Transportation, or
the U.S. Coast Guard, and individuals applying for trusted traveler programs." [1]
ATA supports this new interpretation which will greatly expand the number of individuals in the coming years who apply and pay for a STA and TWIC card. As more
TWIC cards are issued, the establishment of the TWIC as the single, national, uniform credential becomes more critical in order to reduce inefficiencies and lift the
burden of undergoing duplicative background checks and obtaining multiple credentials.

———

RESPONSE TO WRITTEN QUESTIONS SUBMITTED BY HON. DEB FISCHER TO
CHRIS SPEAR

Question 1. Mr. Spear, what type of policies would a Security Threat Assessment
include, in your opinion? In addition to a single credentialing system, what other
policies would streamline the security process without degrading our security?

———

[1] 81 *Federal Register* No. 188; 66671–66672; *https://www.gpo.gov/fdsys/pkg/FR-2016-09-28/
pdf/2016-23370.pdf*

Answer. Currently, the Security Threat Assessment associated with the TWIC and HME requires a FBI criminal history records check, a check against the Terrorist Screening Database, proof of citizenship or immigration status, and proof of identity. As far as the industry is concerned, these checks are sufficient in determining whether an individual poses a threat to national security.

Although a single credentialing process would maximize efficiency while maintaining security, there are other ways to streamline the process. The first would be better communication. The Department of Homeland Security was created by the Homeland Security Act of 2002. This Act brought 22 Federal agencies underneath this new cabinet level department. We believe the department has worked through a number of early concerns, but the industry still faces the situation of being faced with a number of agencies regulating security.

If a driver is screened for a TWIC card, that screening should work for an HME. The background check information used for that screening should not be different, if that driver wanted to apply for TSA precheck, for personal travel. Should there be a reason that a TSA officer does not recognize that the TWIC can be used to board an airplane? The agencies should coordinate their efforts, to minimize overlap and reduce customer frustration. The ability to immediately verify an applicant has been cleared and does not pose a security risk to the Pipelines and Hazardous Materials Administration, should allow for an expedited clearance with the Federal Aviation Administration. Those databases should be able to communicate with one another.

Record keeping is another concern when it comes to streamlining the process. Every five years a new set of fingerprints must be taken to receive a TWIC. According to the Department of Homeland Security Privacy Impact Assessment for the Transportation Worker's Identification Credential,[2] biometric records are retained on an individual while they remain an active TWIC card holder. Upon expiration of the TWIC, those records are destroyed. ATA believes that if that individual would like to continue to transport commodities to port facilities and renew their TWIC, the records should not be destroyed but be retained for the length of the renewal.

Question 2. You mentioned in your written testimony concerns about the GAO's recommendations for "alternative" credentialing methods, including the potential for a decentralized system (whereby each entity has its own port security systems). Can you elaborate further on these concerns?

Answer. A decentralized approach would be disastrous from both an operational and a cost standpoint. Allowing states and localities or individual facilities throughout the country to establish their own STA requirements and issue separate credentials could create confusion regarding site-specific access requirements, especially for those transportation workers who operate at multiple Maritime Transportation Security Act (MTSA) regulated facilities. Furthermore, a decentralized approach would only add to the costs already imposed on motor carriers and drivers today. While establishing additional requirements and credentials for access may be a boon for cash-strapped states and localities, requiring a driver who holds a valid TWIC card to undergo duplicative STAs would waste government resources and create an increasingly burdensome and inefficient operating environment without enhancing security. For these reasons, ATA continues to support the "one credential or screening, many uses" policy that Congress envisioned when creating the TWIC nearly fifteen years ago.

Question 3. What are your thoughts on the United States Coast Guard's (USCG) August 2016 final rule that will require high-risk category facilities and a vessel to incorporate an electronic TWIC validation process, which includes a biometric check for high-risk category facilities and a vessel, prior to entry into a secured area?

Answer. In the final rule, the Coast Guard only requires ports designated as "Risk A" facilities to install TWIC readers at access points to secure areas. Facilities not designated as "Risk A" facilities are not required to install readers, but are required to continue visually inspecting TWICs. Although ATA and its members support the use of such risk-based approaches in developing security regulations, in this particular situation, we are concerned about the lack of uniformity in implementing TWIC readers throughout all MTSA-regulated facilities.

For one, the lack of a uniform access process across MTSA-regulated facilities could create delays resulting from uncertainty or unfamiliarity with site-specific entry verification and inspection processes, especially among commercial drivers who service multiple ports during their operations. Secondly, installing TWIC read-

---

[2] U.S. Department of Homeland Security. *Privacy Impact Assessment for the Transportation Workers Identification Credential Program,* Oct. 5, 2007. Available at: *https://www.dhs.gov/xlibrary/assets/privacy/privacy ▪ pia ▪ twic09.pdf*

ers at additional MTSA-regulated facilities would eliminate the potential for subjectivity by personnel visually inspecting TWICs at entry points. Since readers to authenticate the card's validity, as well as the driver's identity and status, will not be available at over 95 percent of MTSA-regulated facilities, the overall security goal of the TWIC card is undermined. Finally, motor carriers and commercial drivers have invested heavily in applying and paying for what was promised to be a high-tech, secure credential designed to be operated in conjunction with electronic readers. In reality, however, what they have functionally paid for is an expensive "flash pass," since most facilities will not have readers installed to make use of the card's full potential.

ATA believes expanding the scope of the requirement to additional MTSA-regulated facilities will further our shared goal of protecting our Nation's critical transportation infrastructure, reduce confusion at port secure entry points, and fulfill the promise of the TWIC card program.

Question 4. The August 2016 TWIC reader rule also states that, while not required, a maritime operator can utilize electronic TWIC inspection on a voluntary basis if they feel that this provides an additional level of security protection—and many have chosen to incorporate TWIC electronic readers into their USCG facility security plans. Are you seeing the biometric check being utilized beyond the category facilities that will be subject to USCG Final Rule?

Answer. It is encouraging to hear that some operators recognize the security and economic benefits that will come from installing TWIC readers and have chosen to do so voluntarily. However, without a requirement to install the TWIC readers, the vast majority of facilities will continue to rely on subjective visual inspections that will leave them vulnerable to security threats, undermining the goal of the TWIC program and endangering critical infrastructure.

———

RESPONSE TO WRITTEN QUESTIONS SUBMITTED BY HON. CORY BOOKER TO CHRIS SPEAR

Question 1. The Federal Government has a vital role in ensuring that freight flow is not inhibited by a lack of security resources.

In order for our ports to perform efficiently, U.S. Customs and Border Protection (CBP) must be adequately funded and staffed. In 2015, when CBP was last funded to hire additional staff, only 20 of 2,000 staff were assigned to seaports. In addition to the obvious implications for homeland security, this is also a supply chain problem. When vessels cannot efficiently move through the customs process, the delays can ripple throughout our Nation's supply chain.

Although there is no single solution to port congestion, the gap in Federal investment is an issue that we have the ability to address.

What can Congress do to better match resources with the need to secure our supply chain?

Answer. First, there is no replacement for adequate investment in our Nation's freight infrastructure, including our highways and ports. Without it, the issues we face in terms of congestion and security concerns will only grow, exacerbating already unacceptable challenges for the trucking industry. You are correct that the Federal Government has a vital role in ensuring that freight flows are not inhibited by lack of resources and we urge the Congress to continue pushing for ways to increase investment in our Nation's transportation infrastructure.

In the current environment of scarce Federal resources and heightened security we must utilize the programs we have in place to maintain the efficient movement of goods and secure the supply chain. The SAFE Port Act of 2006 mandated that all agencies which require documentation for the clearing or licensing the importation and exportation of cargo to participate in ITDS (International Trade Data System).[1]

ATA has long supported the development of ITDS to provide a single window for all government agencies to gather data to clear cargo entering the U.S. Presidential Executive Order 13659, issued on February 2014 established specific guidelines and timelines for all impacted government agencies to be ready to launch ITDS by December 2016. The automated commercial environment (ACE) is the platform utilized by ITDS and will eventually become a one stop shop for international trade. Like many large undertakings, there are unforeseen mishaps and delays on implementation. However, no progress has ever been gained without setbacks. When ACE/ITDS is fully functional, it will allow for enhanced safety and security, by providing visibility to additional data and automated communications between govern-

[1]U.S. Customs and Border Protection. International Trade Data System: Fact Sheet Available at: *https://www.cbp.gov/sites/default/files/documents/itds█capab█2.pdf*

ment agencies, as well as an increase in throughput by harmonization of information of international shippers that are utilized by CBP and other PGAs.

Congress can assist the supply chain community by remaining vigilant, holding the agencies accountable for maintaining deadlines, and working with industry stakeholders to discover any inefficiencies or achievements during the implementation process.

Question 2. The Transportation Worker Identification Credential—known as TWIC—is issued by TSA to prevent unauthorized access to ports and other maritime facilities. The TWIC program has faced many criticisms; including several Government Accountability Office reviews that found serious problems with the program that prevented the agency from detecting fraud.

A recent DHS Inspector General report found that similar issues still exist with the TWIC program at TSA. For example, the report found that fraud detection continues to be an issue and that TWICs may be issued even when questionable circumstances exist.

While the program has faced many criticisms, there have been significant security improvements at the ports. Beyond the TWIC program, what other actions are critical to securing ports?

Answer. Operational gridlock caused by systemic port congestion is now an all too common occurrence at America's largest port complexes. The resulting inefficient, time consuming and costly freight transport process also serves to undermine efforts to better secure critical port facilities. Until operational data is routinely collected and analyzed regarding cargo loading and unloading, terminal gate and truck turn times, container processing times, equipment availability etc., port and stakeholder management will be unable to modify and improve port operational performance. As a result, many key port complexes will continue to operate at less than optimum levels and in the resulting congestion, confusion and operational delays will continue to operate in an environment that undercuts security programs centered on maintaining a high degree of situational awareness and watchfulness.

The 2016 FAST Act included provisions that were intended to identify and improve port operational data collection and use under the jurisdictional leadership of DOT and the Bureau of Transportation Statistics (BTS). Unfortunately, the mandated collaborative efforts of the FAST Act's Port Performance Freight Statistics Working Group have so far been unable to collect the types of and sufficient data for the port operational database which can be used to better analyze and modify-manage port activities that creates better value for the public and all port stakeholders, including and especially the trucking industry. While the Working Group continues to meet, failure to come together and develop this database negatively impacts all stakeholders, including government officials seeking to address port challenges in a government and industry stake holders work together to create this data base, congestion and delays will continue in the port freight sector and implementation of security programs will never fully be reached.

Question 3. What role does technology play in improving port security?

Answer. Technology is a critical and essential component to the safety and security of all port facilities. With respect to technology, port facilities and the trucking industry, TWIC readers are a key example of how technology and the trucking industry interact on a daily basis in support of security and efficiency at the entrances to many port facilities.

Although, as previously noted in my testimony, TWIC readers are not required at every port, many port facilities use hand held and stationary TWIC readers as an added layer of security. The TWIC card on its own, amounts to a tamper-resistant, biometric and very expensive flash pass. Upon entry to a facility, there is only a visual verification of the person presenting the credential. In facilities that use TWIC readers, there is confirmation that:

(A) The person presenting the card is verified by fingerprint analysis;

(B) The card is authentic and issued by TSA; and

(C) The card has not been revoked or suspended.

ATA has long supported the use of the TWIC with the enhanced technology of the TWIC readers at port facilities to better ensure the safety and security of these critical locations to national security.

RESPONSE TO WRITTEN QUESTION SUBMITTED BY HON. JOHN THUNE TO
ANTHONY STRAQUADINE, JR.

Question. Mr. Straquadine, I understand the pipelines have worked with TSA to educate their inspectors and that the pipeline industry is satisfied with the overall relationship with TSA. Can you speak to what is making this relationship successful?

Answer. The relationship between the pipeline industry and TSA began very well. Much of the staff at TSA's Pipeline branch had familiarity with the pipeline industry by either having experience at NTSB, PHMSA or the pipeline industry itself. Many of the original visits by TSA to over 100 facilities were very informative to both the industry and TSA personnel. They shared a common goal of increased security and resiliency. Performance based goals with real world implementations are key to keep the focus on continuous improvement. Many of the lessons learned in these assessments were shared in combined TSA annual workshops that had significant participation from industry security professionals. This allowed not only the visited facilities to benefit from the common TSA assessments, but these lessons learned being communicated more widely to the industry.

While there have been reorganizations within the TSA, we have kept that cooperative attitude and have welcomed new staff that have a more diverse responsibility under the TSA management structure. The pipeline industry understands that TSA is working to add additional staff specific to this sector and we look forward to continued collaborative efforts with the agency.

Alliance Pipeline has specifically adopted proactive outreach efforts to build and maintain our relationship with the TSA. This works because it is not an adversarial or regulatory one, but rather, a collaborative approach with the agency. This relationship works well as we discuss sharing threat information and industry response efforts (such as the voluntary Cybersecurity Architecture Review discussed in my Subcommittee testimony).

Alliance Pipeline has also obtained the appropriate level of security clearances for key staff to ensure certain classified threat information can be shared by TSA on a timely basis. This has resulted in ongoing threat related briefings and updates related to our industry/region specific threats.

———

RESPONSE TO WRITTEN QUESTIONS SUBMITTED BY HON. DEB FISCHER TO
ANTHONY STRAQUADINE, JR.

Question 1. Mr. Straquadine, in your written testimony you described another type of security threat to our Nation's pipeline system, "political" security threats. Can you elaborate on this risk and how pipeline operators are working to address this challenge?

Answer. Congress anticipated that there may be security concerns due to threats by outside parties and it directed the Department of Transportation—Pipelines and Hazardous Material Safety Administration (PHMSA) to develop regulations. This resulted in the establishment of a PHMSA regulation addressing injuries or destruction of a pipeline facility. In general, PHMSA has regulatory authority over pipeline companies, but there are two exceptions in their regulations, which include: Excavators who damage a pipeline and the aforementioned "political" security threat activity. The following are PHMSA specific penalties:

§ 190.291 Criminal penalties generally.

(a) Any person who willfully and knowingly violates a provision of 49 U.S.C. 60101 et seq. or any regulation or order issued thereunder will upon conviction be subject to a fine under title 18, United States Code, and imprisonment for not more than five years, or both, for each offense.

(b) Any person who willfully and knowingly injures or destroys, or attempts to injure or destroy, any interstate transmission facility, any interstate pipeline facility, or any intrastate pipeline facility used in interstate or foreign commerce or in any activity affecting interstate or foreign commerce (as those terms are defined in 49 U.S.C. 60101 et seq.) will, upon conviction, be subject to a fine under title 18, United States Code, imprisonment for a term not to exceed 20 years, or both, for each offense.

(c) Any person who willfully and knowingly defaces, damages, removes, or destroys any pipeline sign, right-of-way marker, or marine buoy required by 49 U.S.C. 60101 et seq. or any regulation or order issued thereunder will, upon conviction, be subject to a fine under title 18, United States Code, imprisonment for a term not to exceed 1 year, or both, for each offense.

PHMSA has struggled with these particular enforcement requirements for excavators. The TSA which is no longer part of the Department of Transportation has no regulatory or enforcement authority. The other branches of the Department of Homeland Security (DHS) do not typically deal in the enforcement matters. This leads then to the Federal Bureau of Investigation (FBI) which has investigative authority, and the prosecutorial responsibilities of the Department of Justice (DOJ). In recently reported pipeline incidents, clear evidence was available about the in- tended actions (typically documented on social media), but it was difficult for the FBI to respond quickly to gather the threat related information. While some of this evidence was gathered, there was reluctance by the DOJ to move forward on indict- ments based on the PHMSA authority. Rather, the specific pipeline companies and local authorities are resorting to local statutes concerning criminal trespass.

The security posture of many critical facilities is founded on a deterrence strategy based on enforcement of penalties. Operators, local officials and the FBI gather evidence about the potential crimes but the enforcement is under the purview of the DOJ.

What are we doing to help? We are:

- Trying to educate disparate parts of the Federal Government as to the problem and assist in cross communication on the issue.
- Mobilizing our staff, neighbors, security equipment and consultants to correctly and quickly capture information for these cases.
- Trying to understand why there is a reluctance to prosecute these individuals and assist in removing these impediments for Federal agencies.
- Coordinating with regulatory agencies to improve warning signs at physical locations to emphasize the severe penalties for uninformed trespassers. (However, this effort does not inhibit informed perpetrators).

Question 2. The TSA administrator previously testified that the agency spends just 3 percent of its budget on surface transportation programs. Several of you mentioned the lack of interaction with TSA staff in your statements. Can you tell us about your interactions on a regular basis with TSA officials and staff? How could Congress improve TSA interactions and guidance to surface transportation operators?

Answer. The pipeline industry supports TSA's efforts to fill open management positions related to our industry sector. We have invited the TSA to participate in industry tabletop exercises and reviews. Our sector has been helping to review potential improvements to the TSA Security Guidelines.

Alliance Pipeline staff with security clearance stay in routine contact on the State and Federal level with TSA pipeline security personnel and have access to the approved security databases, appropriate to our industry. Alliance also supports TSA participation in industry related exercises and reviews with TSA pipeline personnel in our operating region.

Question 3. The August 2016 TWIC reader rule also states that, while not required, a maritime operator can utilize electronic TWIC inspection on a voluntary basis if they feel that this provides an additional level of security protection—and many have chosen to incorporate TWIC electronic readers into their USCG facility security plans. Are you seeing the biometric check being utilized beyond the category facilities that will be subject to USCG Final Rule?

Answer. The U.S. Coast Guard (USCG) initiated this TWIC card effort, and while there may be some applicability to overall security efforts, the inflexibility and cost of implementing this program seems to be inhibiting wider use other than what is specifically mandated by the Coast Guard. Applying the TWIC identification system outside of USCG facilities seems to be faltering and other solutions that are more flexible for more industries (*e.g.,* electric utility industry) seem to be gaining traction in a one-stop personnel identification process.

Alliance Pipeline specifically comments that the TWIC reader program is an available security tool for USCG facilities and suggests that broad adoption of this program for non-USCG facilities would NOT enhance the security for land-based pipeline facilities. The security infrastructure, training and company-level enforcement tools needed to deploy this program for the pipeline industry as a whole would impose an undo resource and financial burden on our industry with little to no benefit to our security profile.

RESPONSE TO WRITTEN QUESTIONS SUBMITTED BY HON. CORY BOOKER TO ANTHONY STRAQUADINE, JR.

Question 1. The Federal Government has a vital role in ensuring that freight flow is not inhibited by a lack of security resources.

In order for our ports to perform efficiently, U.S. Customs and Border Protection (CBP) must be adequately funded and staffed. In 2015, when CBP was last funded to hire additional staff, only 20 of 2,000 staff were assigned to seaports. In addition to the obvious implications for homeland security, this is also a supply chain problem. When vessels cannot efficiently move through the customs process, the delays can ripple throughout our Nation's supply chain.

Although there is no single solution to port congestion, the gap in Federal investment is an issue that we have the ability to address.

What can Congress do to better match resources with the need to secure our supply chain?

Answer. Department of Homeland Security (DHS)—Transportation Security Administration (TSA) needs to better match its resource allocation to the actual transportation security threats in each transportation mode. S. 3379 proposed such threat-analysis budgeting for DHS–TSA, and the natural gas pipeline industry would support that approach.

Question 2. As surface transportation assets become increasingly automated and reliant on advanced technologies for their safe operation, they also become more vulnerable to cyber-based attacks. What steps are you taking to ensure that critical infrastructure is protected against a cyberattack?

Answer. Natural gas pipeline systems are operated by using a distributed control network topology with oversight from a centralized Supervisory Control and Data Acquisition (SCADA) system. The independent nodes can operate without the central system operating. Within each node there are backup control systems that will maintain set points. Safety systems and emergency shutdowns are independent of the control systems and are not computer based.

The physical transportation of natural gas occurs at relatively slow speed allowing significant time to respond to changes. Individual pipeline operators may also include multiple system redundancies to limit or minimize potential impacts associated with cyber threats.

As discussed during the December 7, 2016 Subcommittee hearing, Alliance Pipeline participated in a two-day voluntary Cyber Security Architecture Review with members of the Federal Energy Regulatory Commission (FERC)—Office of Energy Infrastructure Security (OEIS) and DHS–TSA's Office of Security Policy and Industry Engagement. This Review was designed to be a collaborative, non-regulatory approach that promotes secure and resilient infrastructure through the sharing of information and best practices. The goal of the Review was to gain a comprehensive understanding of an entity's overall cybersecurity posture, to identify potential areas of concern, and to articulate actionable recommendations and observations that promote positive change to the security posture of the reviewed organization.

The outcome of this Cybersecurity Architecture Review was well received by all parties participating, as Alliance Pipeline received numerous best practice recommendations offered by OEIS and DHS–TSA. Alliance is working to implement recommendations that have been prioritized to ensure ongoing safe and efficient cybersecurity operations. Alliance dedicates attention, expertise and resources to reinforcing and maintaining its cybersecurity measures on a continuing basis.

Question 3. What communication or coordination, if any, have you had with Federal agencies to assist in the prevention of a cyberattack?

Answer. The primary information interface for the natural gas pipeline industry is with the DHS—Industrial Control Systems Cyber Emergency Response Team (ICS–CERT). ICS–CERT's mission is to guide a cohesive effort between government and industry to improve the cybersecurity posture of control systems within the Nation's critical infrastructure. ICS–CERT assists control systems vendors and asset owners/operators to identify security vulnerabilities and develop sound mitigation strategies that strengthen their cybersecurity posture and reduce risk. They work to reduce risks within and across all critical infrastructure sectors by partnering with law enforcement agencies and the intelligence community and coordinating efforts among federal, state, local, and tribal governments and control systems owners, operators, and vendors. Additionally, ICS–CERT collaborates with international and private sector Computer Emergency Response Teams (CERTs) to share control systems-related security incidents and mitigation measures. *https://ics-cert.us-cert.gov/About-Industrial-Control-Systems-Cyber-Emergency-Response-Team*

ICS–CERT partners with members of the control systems community to help develop and vet recommended practices, provide guidance in support of ICS–CERT incident response capability, and participate in leadership working groups to ensure the community's cybersecurity concerns are considered in our products and deliverables.

ICS–CERT facilitates discussions between the Federal Government and the control systems vendor community, establishing relationships that foster a collaborative environment in which to address common control systems cybersecurity issues. ICS–CERT is also developing a suite of tools, which will provide asset owners and operators with the ability to measure the security posture of their control systems environments and to identify the appropriate cybersecurity mitigation measures they should implement.

The natural gas pipeline industry has multiple communication interfaces with both the ICS–CERT and the TSA. Specific incident reporting interface for our industry is via TSA Transportation Security Operations Center (TSOC) and FBI. The TSOC serves as TSA's coordination center for transportation security incidents and operations.

Coordination within industry is also handled via Information Sharing and Analysis Centers (ISACs). In December 2016, the Interstate Natural Gas Association of America announced that its industry sector had joined the Downstream Natural Gas Information Sharing and Analysis Center as part of a continuing effort to enhance the security of its members' physical assets and cyber networks. The Federal Government promotes ISACs and Information Sharing and Analysis Organizations (ISAOs) as a best security practice. They serve as a platform for sharing cyber and physical threat intelligence, incident information, analytics and tools. Critical infrastructure sectors use ISACs to share comprehensive analysis within the sector, with other sectors and with Federal and state governments. More than a dozen ISACs exist in the United States, covering a wide range of industry sectors, including electric, nuclear, financial, telecommunications, information technology and water. The American Gas Association formed the DNG–ISAC in 2014. The DNG–ISAC helps local natural gas utilities and natural gas pipelines throughout the Nation share and access timely, accurate and relevant threat information as part of their commitment to the safe and reliable delivery of natural gas to the more than 177 million Americans who rely on it to meet their daily needs. The DNG–ISAC works closely with other energy-related ISACs. *http://www.ingaa.org/News/PressReleases/31333 .aspx*

In addition to the industry actions referenced above, Alliance Pipeline is committed to maintaining its proactive and collaborative approach with both FERC OEIS and TSA staff related to the recently completed Cybersecurity Architecture Review. Alliance continues to maintain an open dialogue with both FERC OEIS and TSA on this topic to reinforce the actions taken as an outcome of this review and to share best practices.

––––––––

RESPONSE TO WRITTEN QUESTIONS SUBMITTED BY HON. DEB FISCHER TO TOM BELFIORE

Question 1. Mr. Belfiore, I appreciate the multi-layered approach for port security that you outlined in your testimony.

As it relates to technology, how has that strengthened your ability to ensure security in the recent past? What are some of the challenges or risks associated with expanding security technology at ports? Does that increase, for example, the risk of cyberattacks?

Answer. We consider security technology at all of our facilities as a force multiplier, supplementing and at times replacing the need for deployment of human assets. Technology allows for the effective, efficient, and secure movement of cargo through our ports.

In recent years at our port facilities, we have greatly expanded our network of CCTV cameras. The Port Authority also created a "trusted trucker" program known as SEALINK, where we capture data and enroll trucking companies and their drivers to ensure only those having actual business at our ports may enter.

Additionally, to assist with large-scale evacuations of the port, we have deployed a port-wide siren and public address system, variable message signage for evacuation notification, and highway advisory radio to notify truckers.

The challenge to technology we find most is the cost of ownership. Beyond the initial capital outlay, it is important that funds be allocated for continued maintenance and recurrent operator training over the long term. Cyber-attacks of course are a risk to any technology system, but one that we believe can be largely mitigated through an effective cyber defense program. The heavy reliance of the maritime industry on electronic data transmission systems dictates the need for strong and effective cybersecurity.

Question 2. Many have advocated for TWIC to serve as a one stop shop for security credentialing. What do you think of this proposal for other types of infrastructure, such as airports where the Port Authority uses the Secure Identification Display Area program?

Answer. While a singular security credential across multiple modes of transportation is seemingly attractive, we believe the TWIC program would first need to be strengthened (as noted in the DHS IG's report) and reconciled with the SIDA program before it serves as a replacement to SIDA. There are several significant differences between the TWIC program and the SIDA program that would need to be addressed. For example, CFR 1542 governing airport credentials has a more extensive list of disqualifying crimes. Further, the airport credential lookback period for offenses is 10 years while TWIC appears to be 7 years.

Most importantly, the granting of a SIDA credential takes place on-airport by Port Authority security staff with the analysis of identification documents and criminal history records checks performed by the same staff. The level of scrutiny afforded each applicant we believe is superior to that which would be provided at a Federal TWIC office.

Question 3. What are your thoughts on the United States Coast Guard's (USCG) August 2016 final rule that will require high-risk category facilities and a vessel to incorporate an electronic TWIC validation process, which includes a biometric check for high-risk category facilities and a vessel, prior to entry into a secured area?

Answer. We support the USCG effort to require an electronic TWIC validation process and biometric check for entry into the Nation's high-risk category facilities. We are pleased that the USCG followed a risk-based model in assessing the need for these enhancements rather than a "one size fits all" approach.

Question 4. The August 2016 TWIC reader rule also states that, while not required, a maritime operator can utilize electronic TWIC inspection on a voluntary basis if they feel that this provides an additional level of security protection—and many have chosen to incorporate TWIC electronic readers into their USCG facility security plans. Are you seeing the biometric check being utilized beyond the category facilities that will be subject to USCG Final Rule?

Answer. The areas of our port facilities for which the Port Authority has direct security responsibility do not fall into the high-risk category. Nevertheless, we are evaluating the prospect of procuring handheld TWIC biometric readers (similar to those already in use at our airports) for randomized use in our areas and at times where we may assume an elevated security posture.

RESPONSE TO WRITTEN QUESTIONS SUBMITTED BY HON. CORY BOOKER TO
TOM BELFIORE

Question 1. The Federal Government has a vital role in ensuring that freight flow is not inhibited by a lack of security resources.

In order for our ports to perform efficiently, U.S. Customs and Border Protection (CBP) must be adequately funded and staffed. In 2015, when CBP was last funded to hire additional staff, only 20 of 2,000 staff were assigned to seaports. In addition to the obvious implications for homeland security, this is also a supply chain problem. When vessels cannot efficiently move through the customs process, the delays can ripple throughout our Nation's supply chain.

Although there is no single solution to port congestion, the gap in Federal investment is an issue that we have the ability to address.

What can Congress do to better match resources with the need to secure our supply chain?

Answer. U.S. Customs and Border Protection (CBP) has been very creative in trying to manage their expansive mission with limited resources. Most recently, CBP launched a program wherein certain trusted vessels can begin cargo operations before the vessel is officially cleared by CBP. This simple measure ensures that the efficiency of the supply chain is unimpeded by insufficient resources and we applaud CBP for taking those steps. In a similar fashion, CBP's innovative Reimbursable Services Program authorized under Section 481 under the Homeland Security Act of 2002 and amended by the Cross-Border Trade Enhancement Act of 2016 allows for private sector partners to pay for the cost of CBP resources on overtime to ensure that the supply chains can continue to flow uninterrupted. While this is an excellent stop gap measure that can be used in extraordinary situations, it is not sustainable for either the private sector or CBP.

In the Port of New York and New Jersey, the expectation is that when the Bayonne Bridge Navigation Clearance Project is completed later this year, the container terminal operators will need to expand their hours of operation on a regular basis in order to efficiently handle the surges of cargo that are anticipated. While the CBP Port Director and her staff have been extraordinary partners in working with the port community to address anomalies, they simply do not have sufficient resources assigned to the Port to handle longer hours on a sustainable basis to operate the Non-Intrusive Inspection equipment and scan 100 percent of the containers. A few options that Congress may consider are as follows:

- Better allocate the existing and any additional resources based on risk—not just security risk but also economic risk. The container terminals in the Ports of Los Angeles and Long Beach for example are open up to 20 hours a day, 6 days a week, with full CBP staffing, while our terminals are currently open between 8–12 hours a day five days a week. This will put the PONYNJ at a competitive disadvantage in the future.
- Considering the volume of containers that move thru the Radiation Portal Monitors (RPMs) each day and the manpower required to operate them as compared to the relatively low number of alarms that occur, investigate ways to remotely monitor the RPMs and respond to any alarms with a roving "strike team."
- Evaluate alternative locations for where the radiation scanning could take place. While some studies have been done to evaluate spreader bar mounted radiation detection so that the containers are scanned during the normal handling process, it is not clear what the status of those studies are or why they have not been further developed. CBP should also consider other choke points for where the RPMs could be placed so that each terminal doesn't have to have its own dedicated equipment and manpower.

Question 2. The Transportation Worker Identification Credential—known as TWIC—is issued by TSA to prevent unauthorized access to ports and other maritime facilities. The TWIC program has faced many criticisms; including several Government Accountability Office reviews that found serious problems with the program that prevented the agency from detecting fraud.

A recent DHS Inspector General report found that similar issues still exist with the TWIC program at TSA. For example, the report found that fraud detection continues to be an issue and that TWICs may be issued even when questionable circumstances exist.

While the program has faced many criticisms, there have been significant security improvements at the ports. Beyond the TWIC program, what other actions are critical to securing ports?

Answer. Significant security improvements have been made over the last 15 years at our Nation's ports, and specifically within the Port of New York and New Jersey. The successful ability to achieve effective port security has been based on the development and deployment of a layered system of measures that has integrated capabilities of governments and commercial interests in port areas across the various elements:

- national maritime security (securing and monitoring international sea/shipping lanes, and port entry areas)
- vessels/shipping (vessel security plans, safety and security boardings and inspections)
- maritime facilities/port terminals (facility security plans, outfitting and securing, safety & security inspections, drills and exercise)
- cargo (screening, scanning, inspections and securing)
- personnel/terminal workers/truckers (background checks, credentialing, training)
- intermodal mobility within and to and from port facilities (securing, training, inspections, drills and exercises)

Continued funding of the Port Security Grant program at proper levels allows for the diverse and complimentary physical security measures to securing our ports and the over-arching maritime transportation system.

Question 3. What role does technology play in improving port security?

Answer. We consider security technology at all of our facilities as a force multiplier, supplementing and at times replacing the need for deployment of human assets. Technology allows for the effective, efficient, and secure movement of cargo through our ports.

In recent years at our port facilities, we have greatly expanded our network of CCTV cameras. The Port Authority also created a "trusted trucker" program known as SEALINK, where we capture data and enroll trucking companies and their drivers to ensure only those having actual business at our ports may enter. Additionally, to assist with large-scale evacuations of the port, we have deployed a port-wide siren and public address system, variable message signage for evacuation notification, and highway advisory radio to notify truckers.

The challenge to technology we find most is the cost of ownership. Beyond the initial capital outlay, it is important that funds be allocated for continued maintenance and recurrent operator training over the long term.

Question 4. As surface transportation assets become increasingly automated and reliant on advanced technologies for their safe operation, they also become more vulnerable to cyber-based attacks. What steps are you taking to ensure that critical infrastructure is protected against a cyberattack?

Answer. Cyberattacks, of course, are a risk to any technology system, but one that we believe can be largely mitigated through an effective cyber defense program. The heavy reliance of the maritime industry on electronic data transmission systems dictates the need for strong and effective cybersecurity. A few years ago, the Port Authority launched a comprehensive cybersecurity program based on the Federal NIST 800–53 standards and deployed additional cyber defense tools, increased employee awareness and training, and has set out to implement proper computing controls on all of its' critical systems.

Question 5. What communication or coordination, if any, have you had with Federal agencies to assist in the prevention of a cyberattack?

Answer. The Port Authority receives cybersecurity alerts from the DHS Industrial Control Systems Cyber Emergency Response Team (ICS–CERT), DHS United States Computer Emergency Readiness Team (US–CERT), U.S. Secret Service, and DHS National Cybersecurity and Communications Integration, and the FBI. We also frequently meet with the FBI, U.S. Secret Service (quarterly), and DHS National Cybersecurity and Communications Integration Center (monthly) to discuss Cybersecurity related concerns. These entities also communicate to the agency via the Port Authority Police Department members who are assigned to the JTTF.

Æ

59

This page intentionally left blank.

www.ingramcontent.com/pod-product-compliance
Lightning Source LLC
Chambersburg PA
CBHW081417280526
45788CB00009B/3139